ON THE MONEY

THE
NEW YORKER
ON THE MONEY

THE ECONOMY IN CARTOONS
1925-2009

EDITED BY ROBERT MANKOFF

Andrews McMeel
Publishing, LLC
Kansas City • Sydney • London

ISBN-13: 978-0-7407-8490-3
ISBN-10: 0-7407-8490-0

Library of Congress Control Number: 2009924140

09 10 11 12 13 RR3 10 9 8 7 6 5 4 3 2 1

www.andrewsmcmeel.com

ATTENTION: SCHOOLS AND BUSINESSES

Andrews McMeel books are available at quantity discounts with bulk purchase for
educational, business, or sales promotional use. For information, please write to:
Special Sales Department, Andrews McMeel Publishing, LLC,
1130 Walnut Street, Kansas City, Missouri 64106.

CONTENTS

INTRODUCTION

by Malcolm Gladwell

You have in your hands something very strange: a book of cartoons about money from the pages of *The New Yorker*. I say strange because we are a magazine for people for whom money is a secondary concern. The guy at the party talking loudly about how he went all-cash in the fall of 2007 is not one of us. We were not at that party. We were at home rereading *Middlemarch*. On those occasions when this magazine does delve into matters of finance and Wall Street, it is with an anthropologist's distance. So what on earth does *The New Yorker* think about when we think about money? The short answer is that we make jokes about it. But there is also a long answer. (And I would not be a *New Yorker* writer if I did not additionally provide a long answer.)

Once, a long time ago, I attended a corporate retreat of a very large company. It was in one of those resorts tucked away in the middle of nowhere. One of the sessions was a trust-building exercise for the firm's senior executives. A group of eight or so top managers sat around a long conference table and each was asked to tell his life story. The firm's chief financial officer went first. He walked to the front of the room carrying—much to my puzzlement—a laptop. He opened it, launched the PowerPoint program, and put up a slide of an older man. "This is my father," the CFO said. He then clicked through to the second slide. It was of a bottle of whiskey. "My father was an alcoholic," the CFO said. The other executives around the table nodded sympathetically. The presenter went on, baring ever more intimate details about his childhood and family: click, click, click. I missed all of it. I was still stuck on slide one. *PowerPoint?*

There is, of course, nothing wrong with what the CFO was doing. He was not a trained storyteller or even someone, as you can imagine, who was particularly comfortable sharing his inner life with a roomful of his colleagues. He was anxious. PowerPoint is the storytelling tool for those who are not in the storytelling business, and it allowed him to do what he would otherwise have found impossible.

So why was I so stunned? Because it never occurred to me, until that moment, that someone might import a business practice into the realm of the personal. PowerPoint, in my mind, was labeled *work*, not self, and work, I believed, should not contaminate self. "I cannot see much of a future for us going forward," I once overheard a banker tell his soon-to-be ex-girlfriend in a restaurant. Same thing: *going forward?* Was she a 10-K filing? Those of us who do not belong to the business culture do the opposite: we want to import personal practices into the realm of business. We want bosses to be kindly and forgiving. We want corporations to wear a human face. We want financial documents to be written in "plain English." The gap between those on the inside of the capitalist system and those on the outside is sometimes described as a deep philosophical divide, or an irreconcilable struggle between two cultures. It's not. It's a very simple quarrel over the direction of what, in basketball, they call the possession arrow. Do you evaluate work life through the lens of the personal, or personal life through the lens of work?

Let me give you another example: Bernard Madoff. Madoff's stroke of devious brilliance was to manufacture, year in and year out, annual gains that fell like clockwork between 10 and 12 percent. From 1990 to 2005, Madoff claimed to have lost money in only seven out of those 174 months, for a 96 percent "winning" percentage. Since he was making the whole thing up, he could, of course, have mimicked the volatile ride of the hedge-funders: up 50 percent, then 12, then 32, then a "down" year of a 2 percent loss, which presumably would have been even more enticing because 50, 12, 32, and -2 averages out to much better than 12, year in year out. But he didn't. Why? Because he understood what consistency means in personal terms: it means trustworthiness, mastery, competence, safety. He was looking for people who imported personal virtues into the business realm.

On the other side of the equation was Madoff's bête noire, Harry Markopolos, the financial analyst who famously wrote a seventeen-page memo to the SEC in November 2005, accusing Madoff of running the biggest Ponzi scheme in human history. The memo is a work of genius, and it repeatedly returns to what Markopolos believes to be the most compelling prima facie evidence that Madoff was a crook. And what is that fact? *That in the previous 174 months Madoff had declared a loss on just seven occasions.* "Classify this as definitely 'too good to be true!'" Markopolos writes of Madoff's winning streak. "No major league baseball hitter bats .960, no NFL team has ever gone 96 wins and only four losses over a 100-game span, and you can bet everything you own that no money manager is up 96 percent of the months, either." Note that Markopolos was not primarily suspicious of *how much* money Madoff claimed to have made. He was more suspicious of the *pattern* of that alleged moneymaking. Markopolos then tells the SEC about other people on Wall Street who think as he does—a managing director at Goldman Sachs who tells Markopolos his firm doesn't trust Madoff and so refuses to trade with him, a managing director at Citigroup who "can't believe that the SEC hasn't shut down Bernie Madoff yet." What did they know about Madoff? Nothing much. Madoff's operation was a black box. All that was necessary to spark their suspicions was that same unbroken string of winning months. They saw no reason to give Madoff credit for consistency, because consistency is a personal virtue. In their world, great investors were people who fearlessly rode winning streaks and persevered through bull markets—who were, by definition, as inconsistent as the market. Fifty, 12, 32, and -2 they would have believed. Me, I look at that string of numbers and see a manic-depressive.

Is one of these positions better than the other? Not really. The victims of Bernie Madoff would have done well to think of Madoff in business terms, not personal terms. Then again, the traders at AIG, who have cost taxpayers many, many multiples of what Madoff cost the world, would have done well to import a healthy dose of personal virtue into their professional practices. We are not talking about the difference between experts and outsiders. We are talking about differing habits of delusion. If this were a real *New Yorker* article, I would now spend several paragraphs coming up with precisely the right name for these two opposing viewpoints. But it is not, and, besides, you are anxious to get to the cartoons. Let's simplify matters. People who want the world to conform to the principles of business are Realists. People who think the other way around—this is true whether they spend their days parsing sonnets or actuarial tables—are Romantics, and the Romantic position in this case, as you are about to discover, is the comic position.

Let us start with a cartoon from August of 1998 by Barbara Smaller. Two investors stare at a computer screen. One says, "Up a hundred and sixteen points! If only we'd had the foresight to invest ten minutes ago." I laughed out loud at that. But it is not universally funny. There are legions of traders on Wall Street who make their living capitalizing on those kinds of immediate, minute-to-minute swings in the market. The computers that run the trading floors for some Wall Street banks used to be in New Jersey or Pennsylvania, for cost reasons. But with the advent of more sophisticated trading, the banks moved them back to Wall Street, because that meant their orders could be executed more quickly. True story! Traders were losing out on trades to their competitors because of the extra microseconds involved in crossing and recrossing the Hudson River. "I wish we had the foresight to invest fifteen microseconds before!" was what they said to each other, only they weren't joking. Realists really do use the language of experience, reflection, and regret to describe things that happened a microsecond ago. The Romantic spends three hours a week with his shrink regretting things that happened *thirty years* ago. To the Romantic, ten minutes is hilarious.

Or consider the multiple versions, in the pages ahead, of cartoons about investors on Wall Street jumping to their deaths. It's a *New Yorker* cartoon trope, as reliable as the man lying on a psychiatrist's couch. My favorite is from 1956. Two men in their Wall Street office watch a body fly by their window: "Why, that's Prescott! Suppose he knows something we don't know?"

You might reasonably wonder how something as tragic as suicide came to be a staple of *New Yorker* humor. But think about the meaning of the man-jumping-out-a-window-because-of-a-drop-in-the-stock-market scenario. This is not malice or Schadenfreude. The man doing the jumping is the Romantic. He has imported the conventions of unrequited love and depression and irretrievable loss—the conditions of the soul—to prosaic questions of profit and revenue. And the two men in their Wall Street office? They are Realists, rewriting the personal in the language of the professional: they see suicide and think, instantly, of what finance professors like to call "information asymmetry." The Romantic laughs first at himself for seeing personal tragedy in the market and, on his way down, at the Realist for not seeing personal tragedy in the market.

Here's another, from 1982. Two corporate types place a report on their boss's desk: "These projected figures are a figment of our imagination," one of them says. "We hope you like them." Who is talking? It's Prescott again! Now our anguished poet is writing earnings estimates. Here's another—man watching television: "On Wall Street today, news of lower interest rates sent the stock market up, but then the expectation that these rates would be inflationary sent the market down, until the realization that lower rates might stimulate the sluggish economy pushed the market up, before it ultimately went down on fears that an overheated economy would lead to a reimposition of higher interest rates." The Romantic is now a financial-news anchor, parsing Wall Street's random walk with dogged literal-mindedness.

Man listening to the radio: "The third-largest bank in the country announced today that it would jump off the Brooklyn Bridge. Other banks are expected to follow its example."

Do Realists have their own book of cartoons? Maybe. But I'll wager it is nowhere as good as this. The truth is that not everyone gets an equal shot at funny. The comic position is a choice; it is the reward of choosing to see the world in a particular way. Romantics tend not to make fortunes on Wall Street, because to profit in finance you really have to be capable of wondering what made Prescott jump. Romantics cannot do that. But they can laugh, and these days, anyway, that sounds like a pretty good trade-off. Man standing in front of an enormous French château: "I could cry when I think of the years I wasted accumulating money, only to learn that my cheerful disposition is genetic." The Realist can have his château and his tears. We Romantics will take the laugh.

1920s

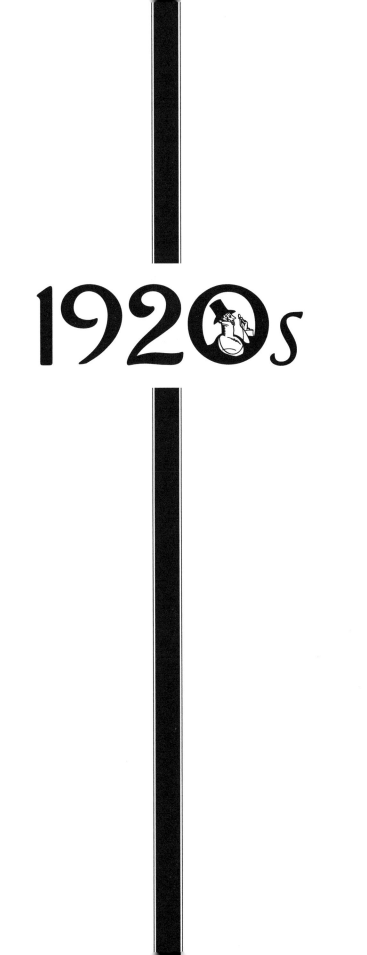

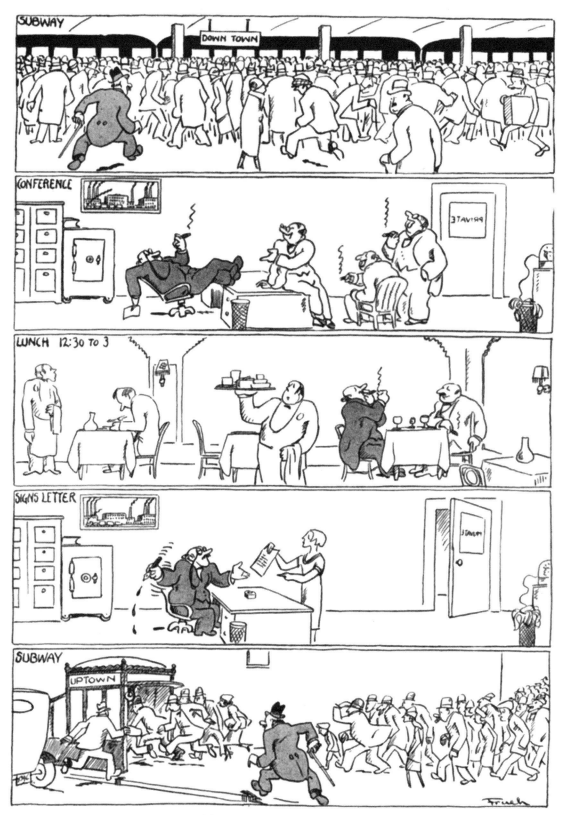

The Busy Business Man's Day

THE STOCK EXCHANGE AS IT REALLY IS

Stock brokers do not gnash their teeth or clasp their hands to their brows or pull each other's hair. They stand about nonchalantly in circles, and are continually passing small pieces of paper to each other which they immediately throw on the floor.

The first buy of the morning is always a white carnation.

The gentleman who undertook to explain the intricacies of the stock exchange to a couple of sightseeing school teachers was somewhat surprised when one of them asked, "But—isn't this the aquarium?"

They take a great deal of interest in each other's hair cuts. The one on the left is about to give an honest opinion.

How a stock broker talks— "An 1/8 for 100—that's a new suit you have on—"

1920s

High position on Wall Street

*"You may quote me as saying: 'I was never so happy
in my life as when a youth and poor.'"*

"I don't suppose you know where Cartier's is?"

*"No imagination, eh? Well, I've got enough imagination
to know how much I'm losing every day by loafing
down here in these damn gondolas."*

"He has no right to look so dumb. He isn't so terribly rich."

"Well, how did you make out today?"
"Fine. I sold twenty thousand dollars'
worth of securities in nine holes."

"Hush, dearie! Don't be noisy in a bank!"

"Say, Doc, do me a favor. Just keep your eye on Consolidated Can Common,
and if she goes bearish tell my broker to sell and get four thousand shares
of P. & Q. Rails Preferred on the usual margin. Thanks."

*"John, there's an installment due tomorrow
and I can't remember whether it's the sixth
on the radio, the fourth on the oil burner,
or the ninth on my operation."*

*"But don't you understand? You're a bear and
you've been cornered by the bulls."*

"Darling, here's the bill from the hospital.
One more installment and the baby's ours."

"Sure, a dime's enough! If you tip too much they just laugh at you."

*"No, I have to stay here and work.
I'm unloading copper."*

"May I see what Steel Common did?"

"Come now, you must thank Uncle William for the nice million dollars."

"Would you sell yourself to lift your father's
mortgage on his cooperative apartment?"

"Well, I'm all for putting the Stock Exchange in its place."

1920s

"You poor fellow! The stock market, I suppose?"
"No, lady, I was always a bum."

1930s

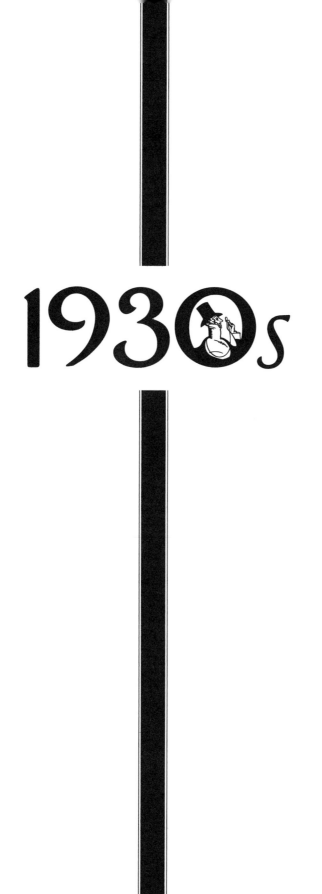

"I'll be down by the economics section. Come in and wake me up about four-thirty."

"They were an ideal pair until he sold her
United Shipping at forty-two and a half."

"Now, you take this depression."
"Huh? What depression?"

"Well, so long.
I'll see you at lunch at the Bankers Club."

"Now we'll know what's what."

"Please, we want to spend for prosperity."

1930s

BIG BUSINESS

*A Board of Directors inspects third-quarter net earnings available for
dividends after deductions for fixed charges, income tax, depreciation, and obsolescence.*

"Er—would it seriously inconvenience you if I withdrew two hundred dollars?"

"Do you realize what it would mean to have a man with Wall Street experience in the business?"

1930s

TURNING OF THE TIDE

A brokerage house receives an order to buy ten shares of Goldman Sachs.

Just around the corner

1930s

"Buyer hesitancy is what's keeping this country back, if you ask me."

"I saw it all coming ten years ago."

1930s

"This year I'm asking everyone
just to give me money."

"I say to hell with the
law of supply and demand."

"We're on a budget."

"I never told her about the Depression. She would have worried."

"I'd like to have about five more, but Albert says we can't buck Wall Street."

*"That's the same man who bought ten copies of
'The Coming American Boom' last summer."*

"He charges $2,500 for a portrait—no extra charge for a child under seven."

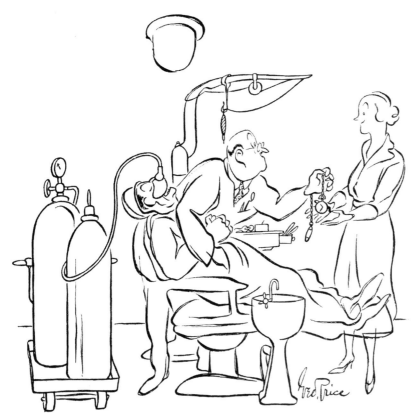

"Now, I'll extract a ten-spot in payment of his last bill."

"There's such a thing, Laura, as carrying this budget business too far."

"Most of them are mysteries to me, but that one on the right gives stock-market averages."

"Mr. John D. Rockefeller, Jr., called this morning, but he had the wrong number."

"My stocks are all going up again. Is that a bad sign?"

1930s

"Well, _whoever_ he is, every time I ring up
a dollar he snatches out thirty cents."

"We say 'recession' here—not 'depression,' Miss Apgar."

"Could I wash my hands while you compound my interest?"

*"Funny thing about Morley—he sacrificed his ideals
and still he doesn't make any money."*

"There are four letters from the Collector
of Internal Revenue this morning,
all much in the same vein."

"... whereas this fellow here advocates a pension
of thirty dollars every day _except_ Thursday."

"By Jove, I'd almost dig into capital for her."

1930s

"Vintage '29. Ah! Steel 261—Can 184—Tel & Tel 310."

"By the way, your broker phoned this morning."

"He's an investor, or speculator, or embezzler—anyway, he's rich."

A Revised Statuary for the City of Tomorrow

"These dreams of yours wherein you find great tubs of money, Mr. Croy—can you describe the spot a little more exactly?"

"Heavens! If you listen to Consumers' Research, you'll never buy anything."

"If it gives you any more trouble, let me know."

1930s

1940s

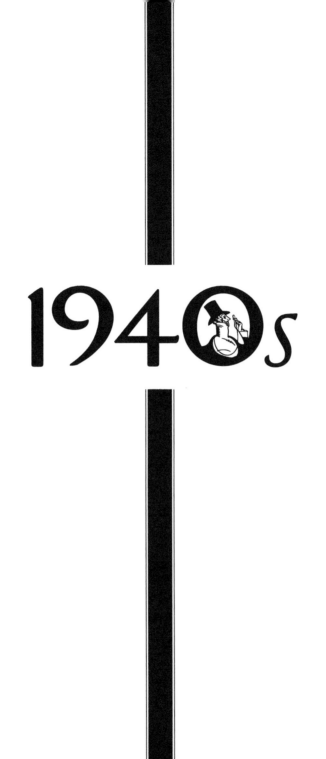

"I'm told that the 1929 crash took everything she had."

"Twenty years on this job, and still she won't listen to me in money matters."

"There's no doubt about it—business simply isn't borrowing money these days."

1940s

"My God, Joe! Now they want to buy it all back."

"I couldn't recommend a safer investment for your money."

1940s

*"We've been terribly cramped since John got to worrying
about inflation and began to convert his assets into <u>things</u>."*

"S-a-a-y, I just happened to think. When <u>this</u> war is over we'll probably draw another bonus."

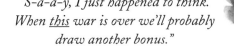

"Why, I understood the government had made provision for dependents."

"We were just making a little ceremony of burning the mortgage."

1940s

*"Ted says the camp is swell. He likes the sergeant and the
other fellows fine, and needs more money for ammunition."*

"But, darling, there were the pay-as-you-go taxes, the deduction for War Bonds, Social Security, group insurance—and I had a small beer."

"Very good, Benson, but how are you going to squeeze in 'Buy More War Bonds'?"

"Damn it! Now I've got to revise my estimated income for 1944."

"So long, Ted, and thanks a billion!"

1940s

"That's all very well, old fellow, but have you ever thought where you will be if <u>deflation</u> comes?"

"Well, one thing—we haven't got much of an inventory problem this year."

"Do you want a hot market tip, Howard? Pacific Northern has just voted an extra dividend."

"You will notice that while we suffered local reverses in cosmetics and lingerie, we drove a deep salient into the enemy's lines in hosiery."

1940s

"Is it patriotic yet to ask for a raise?"

"Thank you very, very much. I don't know how I can ever repay you."

1940s

*"Look at it this way, Simpson. When you ask for a raise,
you're asking our stockholders to take a cut."*

"And now, just before the next depression I want you to
take all my money out of stocks and buy bonds."

"Well, why didn't you earn
as much as you estimated?"

1940s

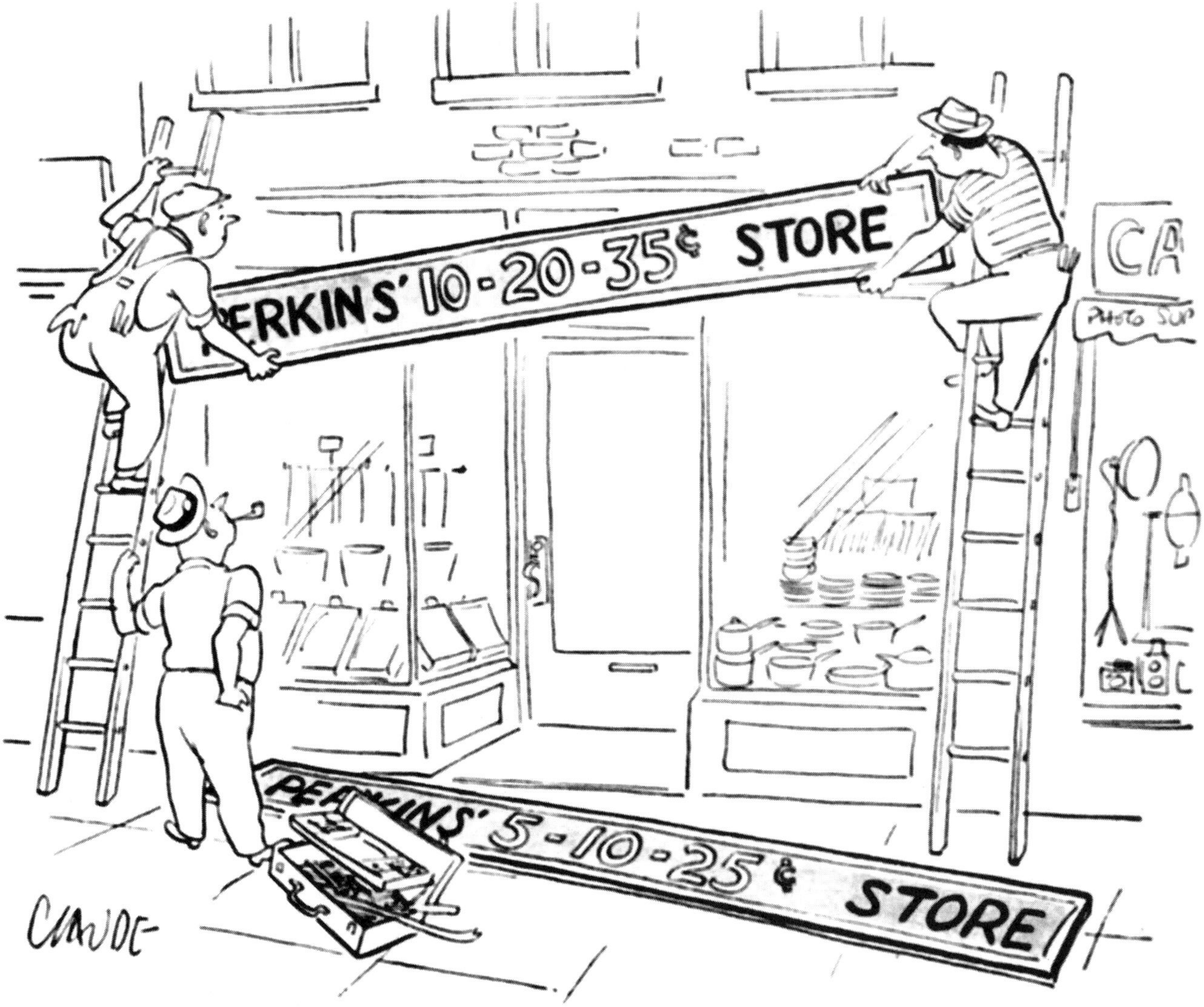
PERKINS' 10-20-35¢ STORE
PERKINS' 5-10-25¢ STORE
CLAUDE

"When you say Merrill, Lynch, Pierce, Fenner and Beane recommend a certain stock, do you mean it's unanimous or just a simple majority?"

"It's completely automatic—washes, rinses, drains itself, and shuts itself off, and this little attachment here writes out the installment check for eight dollars on the first of every month."

"I've brought your lunch, Lester, and, Lester, I've been a patient, uncomplaining wife, but when, in God's name, are you ever going to stop plowing the profits back into the business?"

1940s

"This vicious spiral of rising wages and prices has got to stop somewhere, Fleming, and I'm stopping it with you."

"Don't touch it, Roger! It costs two thousand four hundred and seventy-five dollars."

"Harris, I've cancelled your hospitalization and sick-benefit policy, closed out your old-age retirement account, cleared your case with the union, given proper legal notice to the Unemployment Insurance Bureau, and had a check drawn for your vacation credit, cost-of-living bonus, severance pay, and accumulated salary, including overtime. You're fired!"

"I just had a horrible nightmare. I dreamed that A. T. & T. skipped a dividend."

*"I don't see why they can't.
They're supporting the price of everything else."*

*"Has it occurred to you that if everybody paid
their bills promptly, you'd be out of a job?"*

1950s

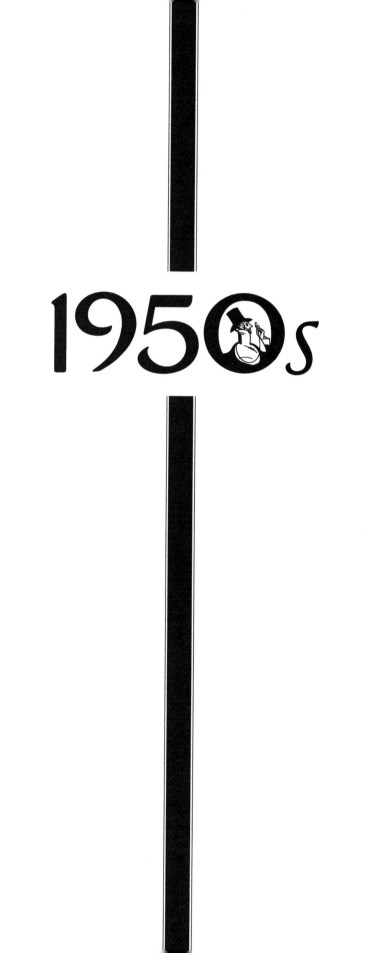

"Other men just lose their money by luck—you got to _figure_ _out_ how to do it."

"How's business?"
"Oh, about the same."

"Hold it, fellows! I'm from the United States
Bureau of Internal Revenue."

"It boils down to this—we haven't had a strike in ten years, so we must have been overpaying them all along."

*"We also think there should be an escalator clause to meet any
cost-of-living increase that may result from the granting of our wage demands."*

*"Of course that's only an estimate.
The actual cost will be somewhat more."*

1950s

"... the stock market moved irregularly lower yesterday in a day of dull trading. Rails and industrials held steady. Brazilian bonds showed a marked flurry in the final hour of trading. Municipal issues were generally ..."

"No, damn it, I want to close one!"

"I know the type. All you'd ever get out of him would be 'We can't afford it'!"

*"It's a pity we didn't meet sooner.
My expense account is already
hopelessly padded."*

*"You don't understand, Dad. It isn't the business itself—that's going great.
But you can't imagine what taxes do to you today."*

"Before you let yourself get carried away with all this, Ethel, let's find out if we can list it as capital gains."

"Remember, now—C.O.D.!"

*"By all means, dear—buy it if you really want it.
We'll find the money for it somehow."*

*"I'm afraid this is good-bye, Miss Woodley.
I've lost the battle for proxies."*

1950s

"What does the total interest add up to? Now come, Mr. Weber, we're not asking you any embarrassing questions, are we?"

"As I see it, your basic problem is the repression of a recession obsession."

"How about a _triple_-your-money-back guarantee?"

"I think my fees will seem less unreasonable to you if you will stop to consider the many long and costly years a doctor must spend to prepare himself, and the tremendous day-by-day expenses a doctor has to face . . ."

"Sure I got a creative urge, but it's satisfied by knowing I could support ten of these guys on the kind of money I make."

"It's such a <u>little</u> country. Couldn't we counteract Communism by just giving everyone a few shares of General Motors?"

"What amazes me is their willingness to submit to that appalling publicity for a mere sixty-four thousand dollars."

"What a wonderful expression! He's caught J.B. right at the peak of the market."

1950s

"Why, that's Prescott! Suppose he
knows something we don't know?"

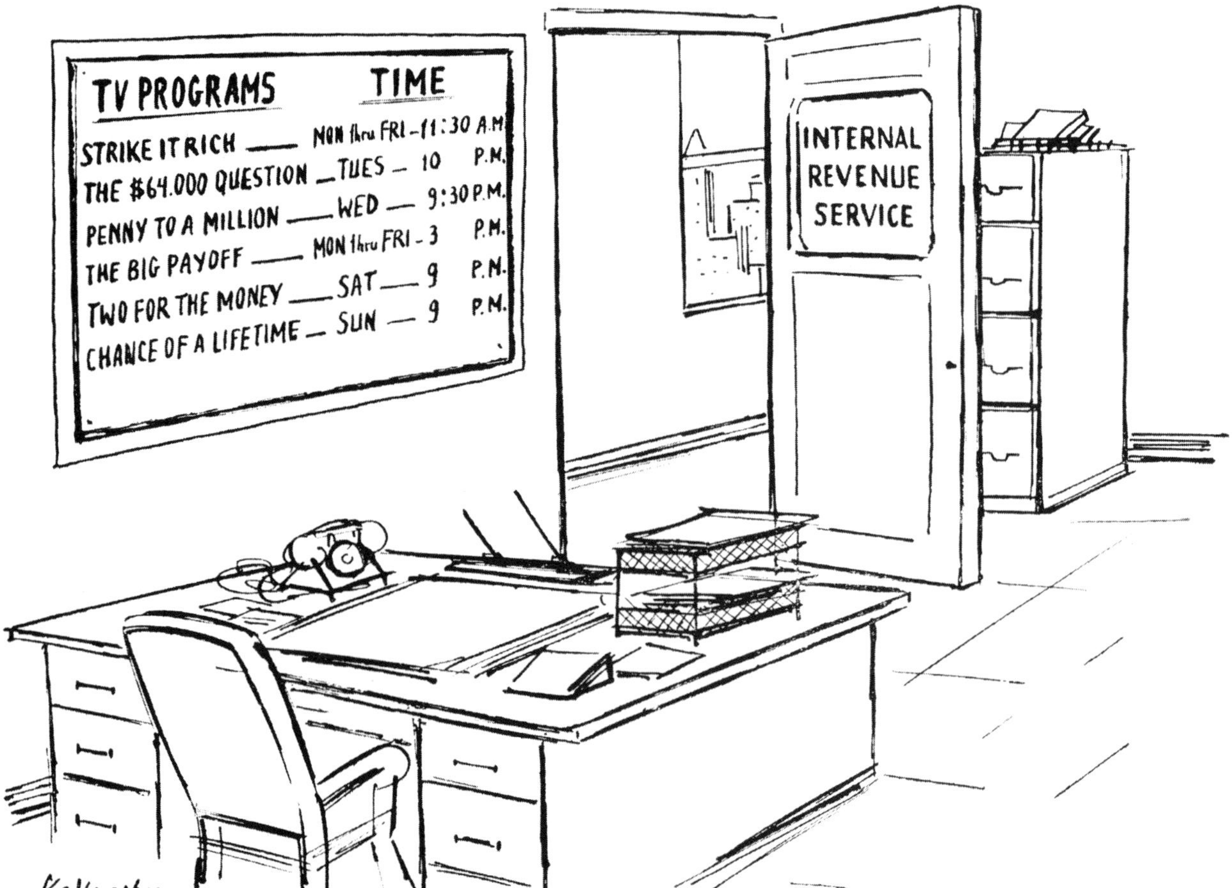
TV PROGRAMS TIME
STRIKE IT RICH — MON thru FRI - 11:30 A.M.
THE $64.000 QUESTION — TUES — 10 P.M.
PENNY TO A MILLION — WED — 9:30 P.M.
THE BIG PAYOFF — MON thru FRI - 3 P.M.
TWO FOR THE MONEY — SAT — 9 P.M.
CHANCE OF A LIFETIME — SUN — 9 P.M.
INTERNAL REVENUE SERVICE
Kovarsky

"Where did the six million go?"

*"I'll tell you what we'll do. We'll allow you eighteen hundred on your old car
and throw in two hundred more toward the cost of lengthening your garage."*

1950s

"I'm forty-six and I'm still driving
one of the 'low-priced three.'"

"To hell with a balanced portfolio.
I want to sell my Fenwick Chemical and sell it _now_."

"I know. Back in the boom days of '27 and '28 things looked pretty black, too.
But I hung right on, and then came October, 1929."

"It happens all the time. Get a research grant from
Rockefeller or Ford, and all of a sudden it's let's live a little."

"It's as simple as two times two.
We're overproduced; they've got to overbuy."

"Here's a 'Wall Street Journal' that appears to be streaked with tears."

"I may or may not need an analyst, but if I do he'd better damn well have a thorough knowledge of the federal tax laws."

1950s

"It's sad that he couldn't have lived to see A. T. & T. at 200 again."

---NERVOUS STOMACH ?   TRY BEP (advt)----

1950s

"*Has it occurred to you that every time we decide to face basic issues,*
all we do is put the house on the market?"

"According to the figures, <u>one</u> thing is clear. I can't live on my salary!"

"Now, please don't recommend any
stock involved directly or indirectly with
blowing us all to kingdom come."

"Lest we be accused of contributing to inflation later on,
let's vote ourselves a good little raise right here and now."

"But Comrade, it's the American inflation!
The ruble just doesn't buy as many top secrets as it used to."

"Harold, can you hear me? Industrials are up, rails are up, coppers are up . . ."

"Now, for God's sake let's try and do <u>one</u> thing right, and not all dump our stock in the corporation at the same time."

"It's happened, Ellen.
We're now living beyond our _second_ income."

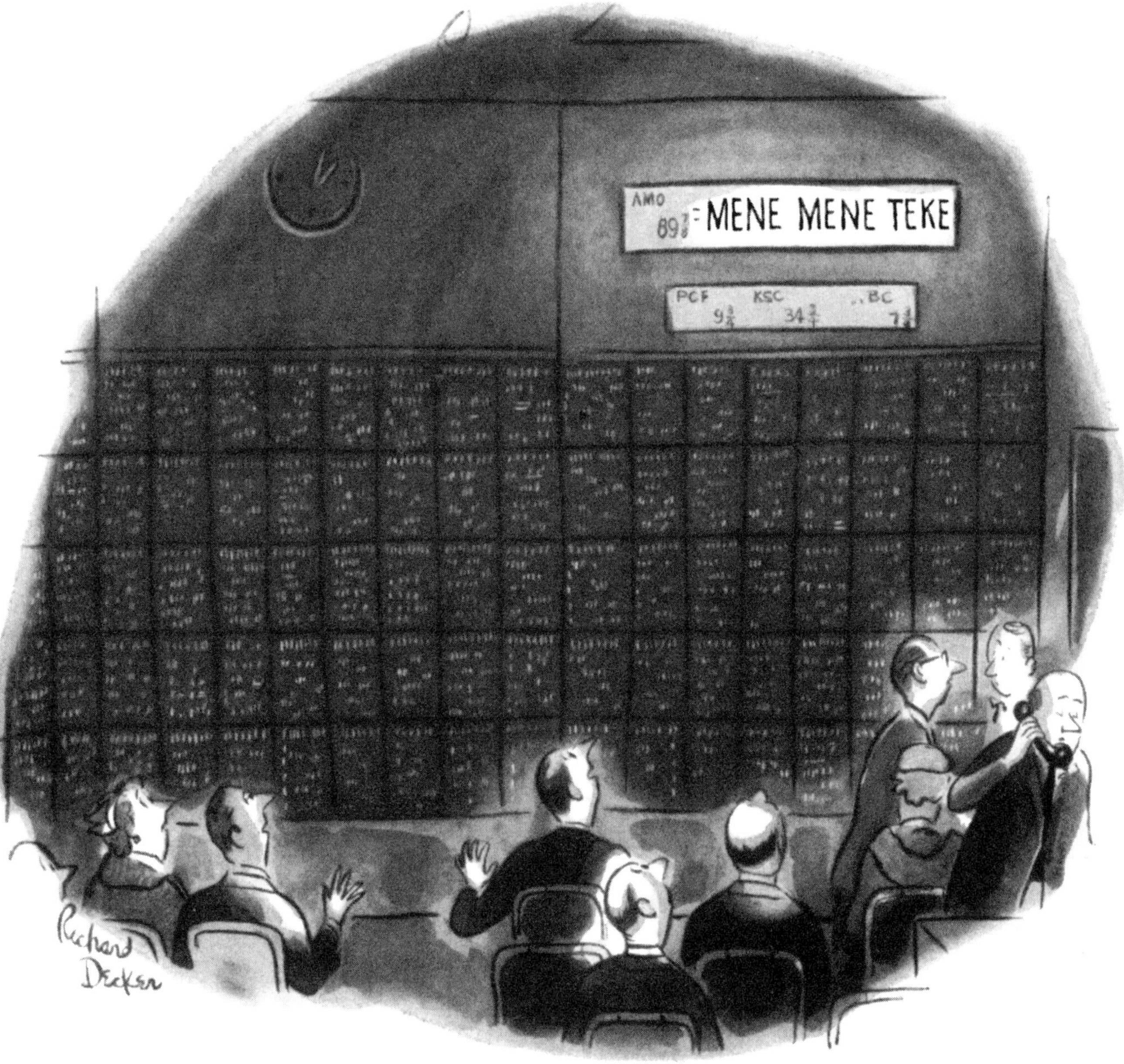
AMO
89⅞ = MENE MENE TEKE
PCF
KSC
BC
Richard Decker

1960s

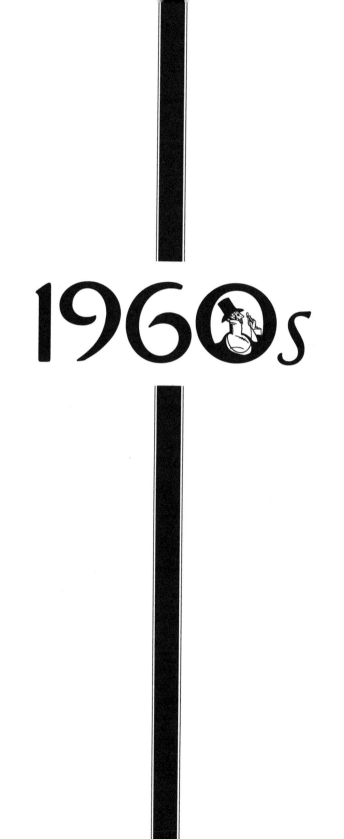

*"So the putt is worth eight thousand dollars to him.
What's your cut? Ten per cent?"*

*"See where I'm pointing? Daddy owns a teeny
little bit of that, and it closed at eighty-six."*

"I admit that Consolidated Aluminum has an attractive starting salary and good fringe benefits,
but Allied Instruments offers all that, plus optional early retirement."

"I'm sticking with old A. T. & T.
Recession or no recession, people
are going to keep right on yacking."

"The cost of living is up again! What the hell kind of a recession is this?"

1960s

"How does one go about getting so fouled up that the government settles for so much on the dollar?"

"Pardon me, but I must have dozed off.
Are we discussing bomb shelters or tax shelters?"

"I certainly hope they don't include _this_
stuff in the gross national product!"

"And another way to help the economy would be to boost teachers' salaries."

*"When Allen Ginsberg has three kids and a mortgage,
maybe I'll listen to what he has to say."*

"Now, for the time breakdown tax-wise, I figure Ed veered away from business to golf for eight minutes; you, Fred, were on your son's algebra block for approximately ten minutes; I then returned to the discussion of the contract . . ."

"Doesn't anyone ever take you out to lunch?"

"In a democracy, a man has a right to ask for credit no matter how many times he's been refused credit."

"The gods are angry!"

"Would that be gross or take-home?"

"Psst! Next Friday's
'Wall Street Journal'?"

"You know, I never thought I'd live to see the day
the Dow-Jones industrial average broke eight hundred."

"If anything should happen to me, Barbara, <u>don't</u> <u>sell</u> <u>Xerox</u>."

"I wonder if it strikes you fellows, as it strikes me,
that all we ever seem to talk about is money."

"And—*they're off!*"

"Who do you figure stands to cash in
on this war against poverty?"

1960s

"Think of it this way.
The whole world is broke, but the United States is less broke."

"Remember, I warned you that only a person with a regular income,
a cash reserve for emergencies, and adequate insurance coverage, plus a surplus,
should buy stocks—and then with the utmost selectivity."

"Gee whiz, Mr. Curtis,
a million dollars isn't old!"

"The hell of it is those punks
pump over fifteen billion dollars
into the economy every year."

1960s

BUY NOW

AT THE ACCEPTED 3.2% INFLATION RATE THE DOLLAR WON'T BUY ANYTHING AT ALL BY 1998

*"What the economy needs is a depression.
Just a small one, and present company excepted, of course."*

*"Gee, Frank, don't you just love living
in a period of extended economic boom?"*

*"But, sir, many analysts consider this only a long-overdue correctional movement,
following which the market will resume its upward course, with a rally
expected to penetrate previous Dow-Jones highs by the year's end."*

"And why, may I ask, do you presume to think your opinions have any validity? Have you ever met a payroll?"

1960s

"Look at it this way, Son. If one of your generation should ever have occasion to call on a stockbroker, he would want to call on one of his own."

"That's tight money for you."

"Well, while we do our part, the folks at home are doing theirs. I see the Dow-Jones is up again."

"I did my job, I grabbed my pile, and yet no voice at eventide has cried 'Well done!'"

"Frank, how ever did you find *this* guru?"

"Gee, Pop, is that the only paternal advice you have for me—never dip into capital?"

"From here on out to the point, it's all new money."

*"Here at Compudata, Inc., Mr. Waycross,
our motto is: Analyze, systemize, computerize,
synthesize, finalize, and make a bundle."*

"The cost of living sure keeps going up and up and up!"

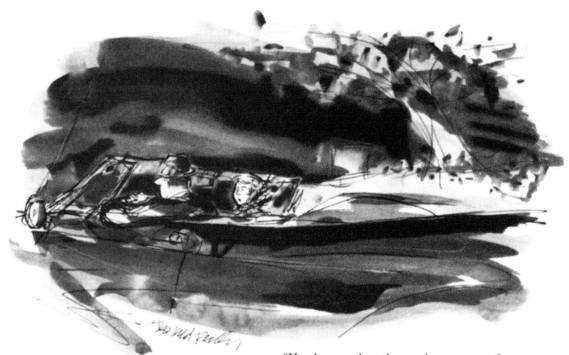

"You know when the magic went out of our marriage, Henry? When we completed our major consumer-purchase decisions."

"Well, our financial worries are over. We're bankrupt."

"For want of a better word, I call my idea 'taxes.'
And here's the way it works."

*"Give us a kiss, young man,
and I'll tell you the top ten growth stocks of 1969."*

"Oh, Joe, not your portfolio again!"

"I think it's a crime to spend billions going to the moon
when repertory theater in this country is more dead than alive."

"Now let's go through the whole thing again—honest mistake by honest mistake."

"Do you know what your generation will see, young fellow?
Your generation will see Dow-Jones industrials break through the two-thousand level."

"I've consolidated all our debts into one low, easy-payment loan,
and now I'm saying good-bye to all our worries."

1970s

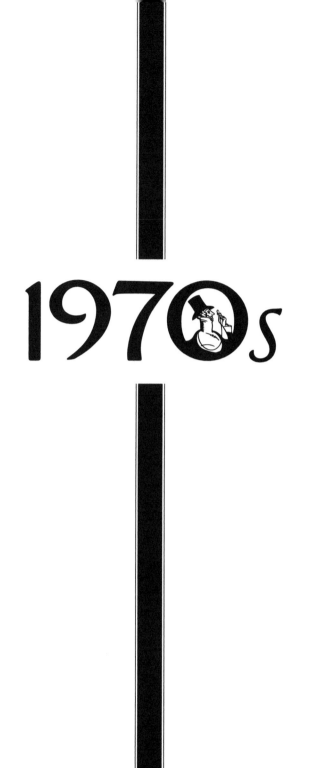

"It's people like you, Mr. Evers, constantly living
beyond your means, getting so hopelessly deeper and deeper
in debt, to whom our industry owes eternal gratitude."

EAT, DRINK,
AND MAKE
MONEY

"That's the stuff that gets us up early in the morning and makes us go to bed before the 'Late Show,' Harold."

BOOTH

"Other folks have to pay taxes, too, Mr. Herndon, so would you please spare us the dramatics!"

"They say to get elected to public office in America one must be rich. Well, my friends, *I'm* rich, I'm *very* rich."

"Are you sure it isn't just a _technical_ rally?"

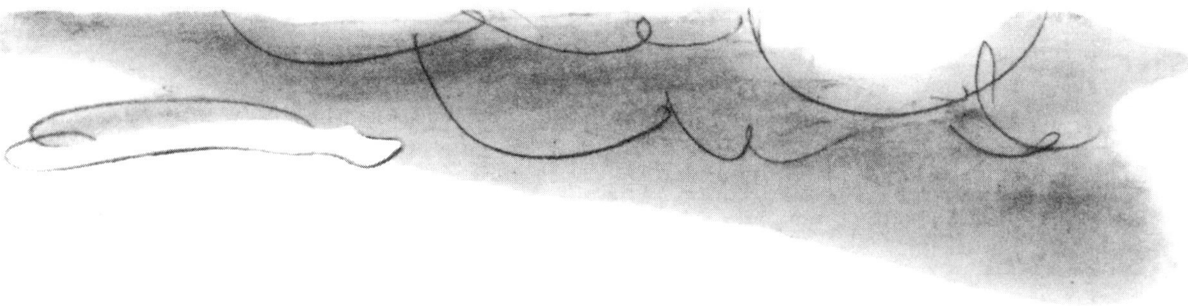

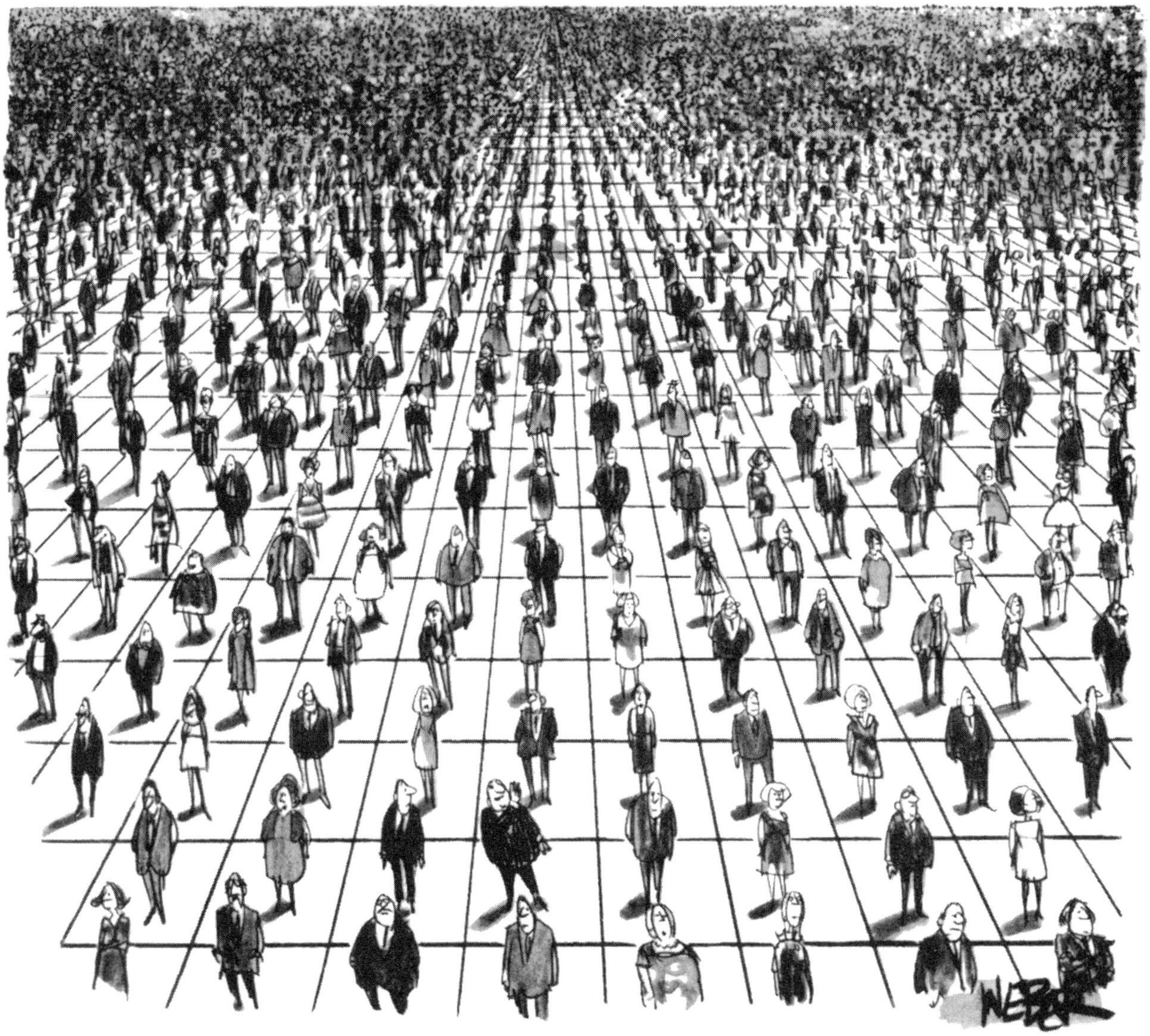

"Excuse me, sir. I am prepared to make you a rather attractive offer for your square."

"*The computer is only a tool.
There will always be a place for unbridled avarice.*"

"*I, for one, am glad the dollar's out of trouble,
because if the <u>dollar's</u> in trouble, then
the <u>dime</u> is certainly in trouble.*"

"For heaven's sake, Bob, can't we walk down the street without your forever fretting about how you could have bought this one for twenty-eight thousand in '58, and that one for thirty-five thousand in '61, and that one for goodness knows what in 1964!"

1970s

"October 29, 1929. It started out a day like any other day.
I had coddled eggs, bacon, and coffee for breakfast.
It was a brisk day. I wore a light topcoat . . ."

"The best things in life may be free,
but the second best can run into real money."

"Come on! It's fifty-four dollars and sixty cents an ounce in Zurich, fifty-four seventy in London, and fifty-four ninety in Frankfurt, and still going up, for all I know!"

"Has the dollar ever been worth <u>more</u> than a dollar?"

1970s

*"Maybe we do bungle the spending of your tax dollar,
but you'll have to admit we do a bang-up job of collecting it."*

"To hell with what the Sierra Club could do with the cost
of a single F-111 fighter plane! Think what _I_ could do
with the cost of a single F-111 fighter plane!"

"Which should I be worrying about?
The wholesale price index, the consumer
price index, or the industrial price index?"

"We make eighteen thousand dollars a year. What do you recommend?"

"They either have more taste than money or more money than taste, but I can never remember which."

"What everyone seems to forget is that A.T. & T., when you come right down to it, is only people—like you and me."

KOREN

"In a large bowl, combine 60¢ of eggs, 45¢ of medium cream, 16¢ of oregano, and 10¢ of
dry mustard. Dip $7.50 of loin pork chops into this mixture and roll in 65¢ of bread crumbs.
Heat 90¢ of peanut oil in a heavy skillet and slowly fry the chops on 94¢ of gas."

1970s

"And here's an extra 'substantial penalty' for
the early withdrawal of your time deposit!"

"I used to make eighty thousand dollars a year as a stockbroker. Give us a little kiss."

"People must be spending their money on something, Jackson, and it's your job to find out what that something is!"

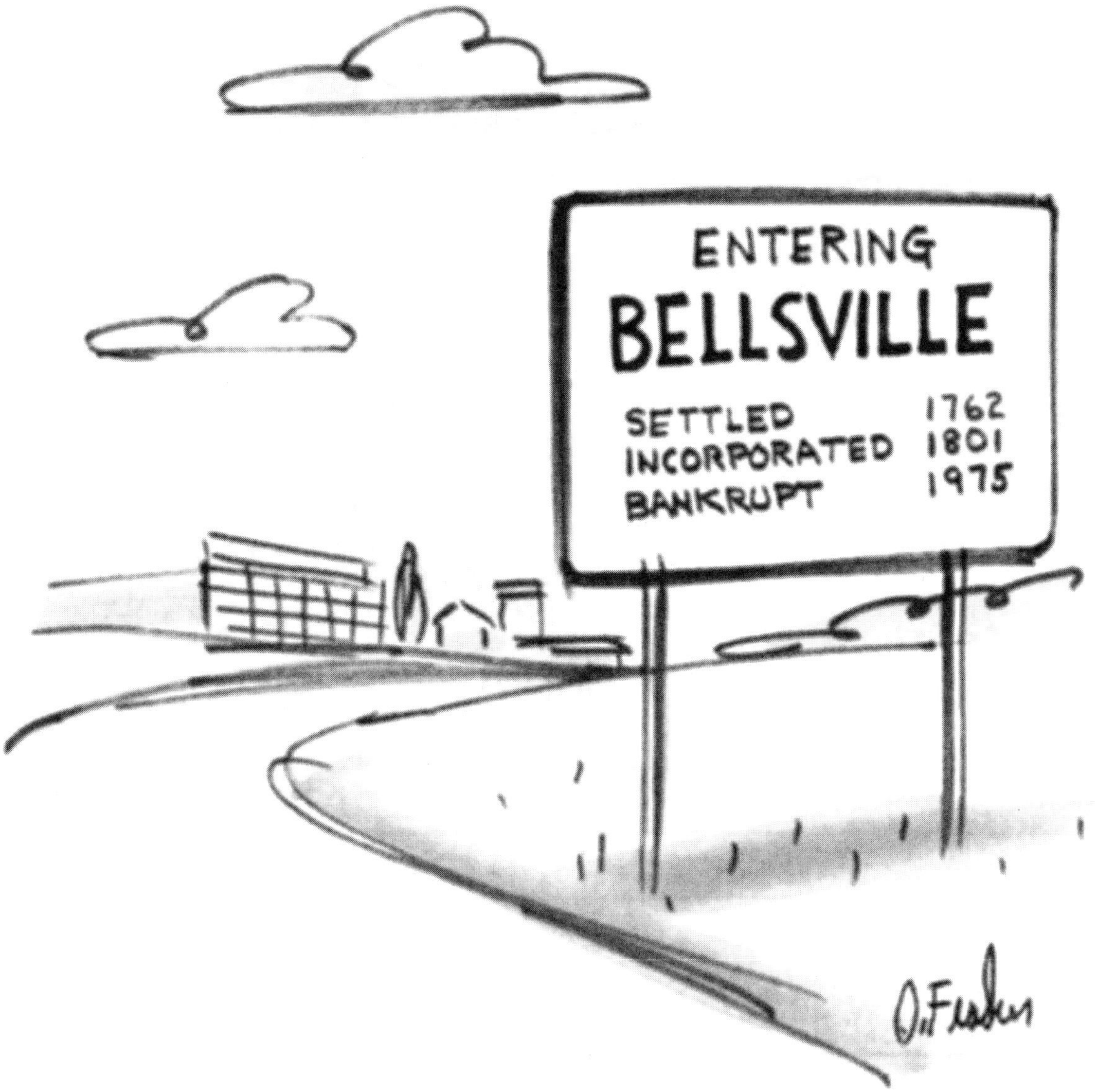
ENTERING
BELLSVILLE
SETTLED 1762
INCORPORATED 1801
BANKRUPT 1975

"Oh, it's great here, all right, but I sort of feel uncomfortable in a place with no budget at all."

"With the budget cuts and then the personnel layoffs, we've had to ask everyone to pitch in."

"Damn it, Felton! Stop passing me money under the table while I'm eating!"

"Just between us, Baxter, now that you're no longer mulcting the funds at Data-Technics, how would you rate them as an investment?"

"He's working on the next generation of fast bucks."

*"Please don't thank me.
I would have accepted a kickback from anyone."*

*"I'll tell you why we were put on
this planet. We were put on this
planet to outperform the market!"*

*"We are gathered here today
to honor all major credit cards."*

1970s

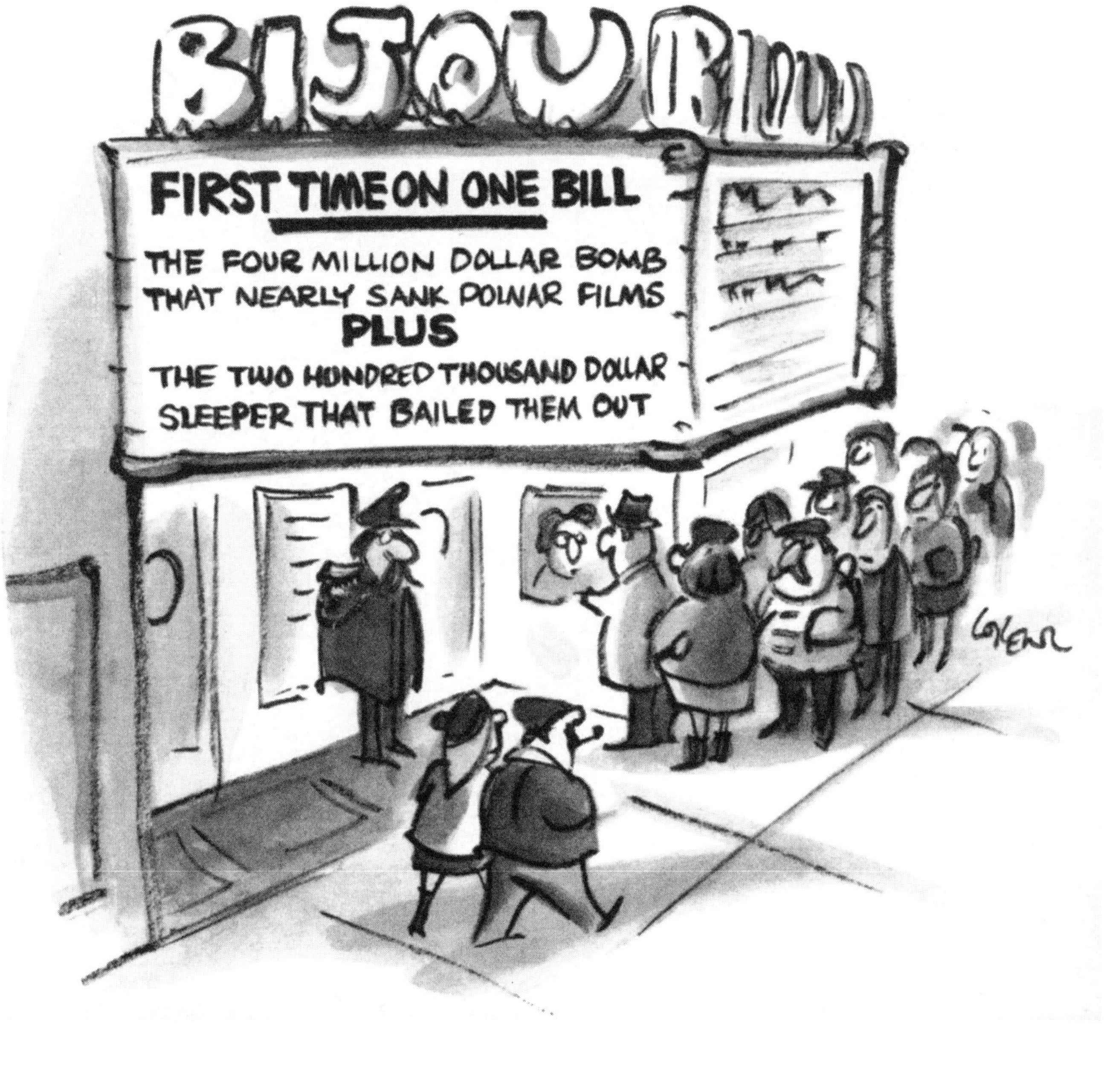
BIJOU
FIRST TIME ON ONE BILL
THE FOUR MILLION DOLLAR BOMB
THAT NEARLY SANK POLNAR FILMS
PLUS
THE TWO HUNDRED THOUSAND DOLLAR
SLEEPER THAT BAILED THEM OUT
LORENZ

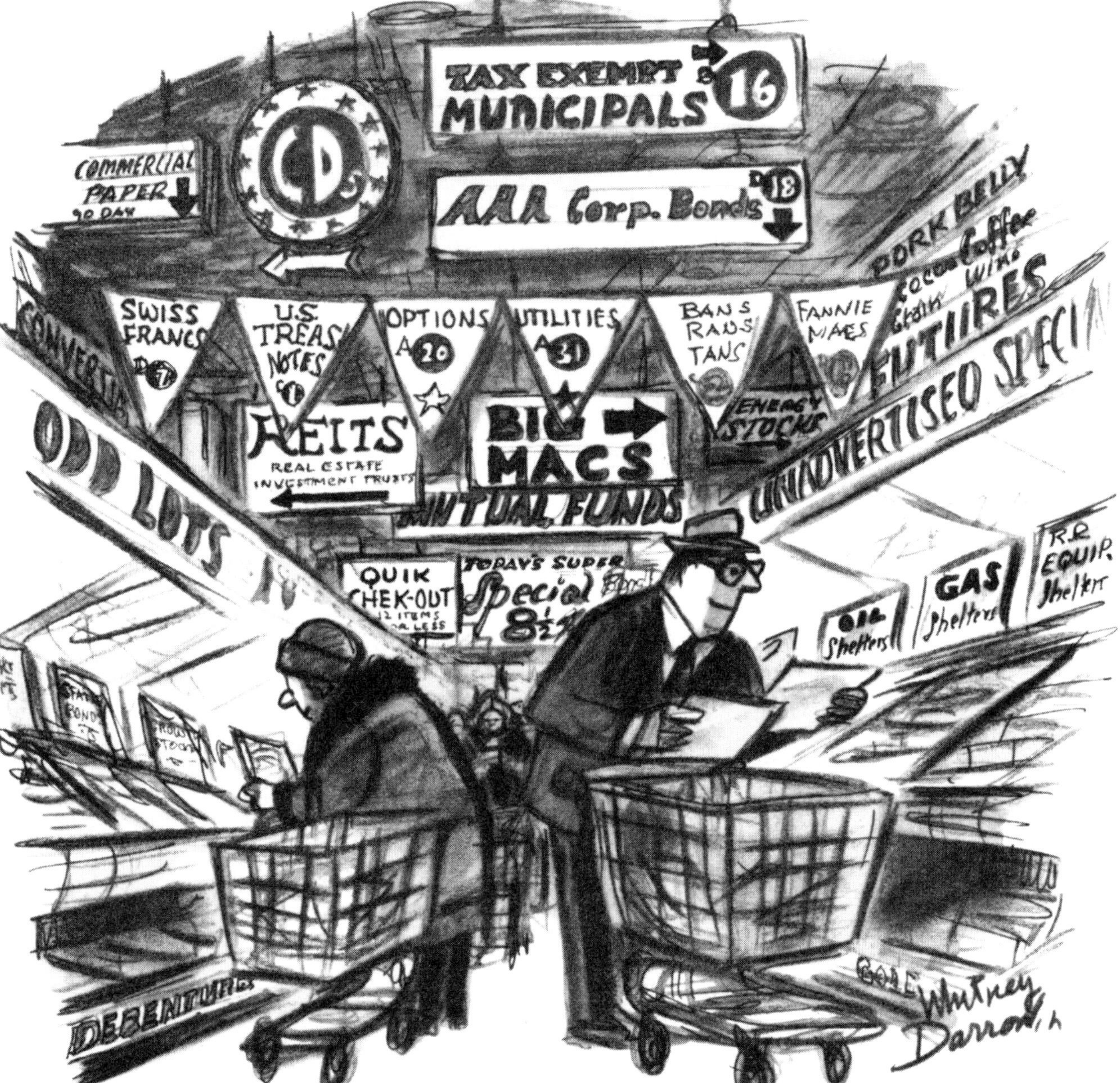

TAX EXEMPT MUNICIPALS
16
C.D.s
COMMERCIAL PAPER 90 DAY
AAA Corp. Bonds
18
PORK BELLY
FUTURES
SWISS FRANCS
U.S. TREAS NOTES
OPTIONS
20
UTILITIES
31
BANS RANS TANS
FANNIE MAES
REITS
REAL ESTATE INVESTMENT TRUSTS
BIG MACS
ENERGY STOCKS
MUTUAL FUNDS
UNADVERTISED SPECI
ODD LOTS
QUIK CHEK-OUT
12 ITEMS OR LESS
TODAY'S SUPER Special 8½
OIL Shelters
GAS Shelters
R.R. EQUIP. Shelter
DEBENTURES
Whitney Darrow, Jr.

"This ten billion, of course, includes bullets."

"Wake me up when the Dow hits a thousand."

"I'm afraid Mr. Koerner is no longer with us.
He was taxed out of existence."

"Our task then, gentlemen, is to persuade the government that the best way to solve a problem <u>still</u> is to just throw money at it."

"Money is life's report card."

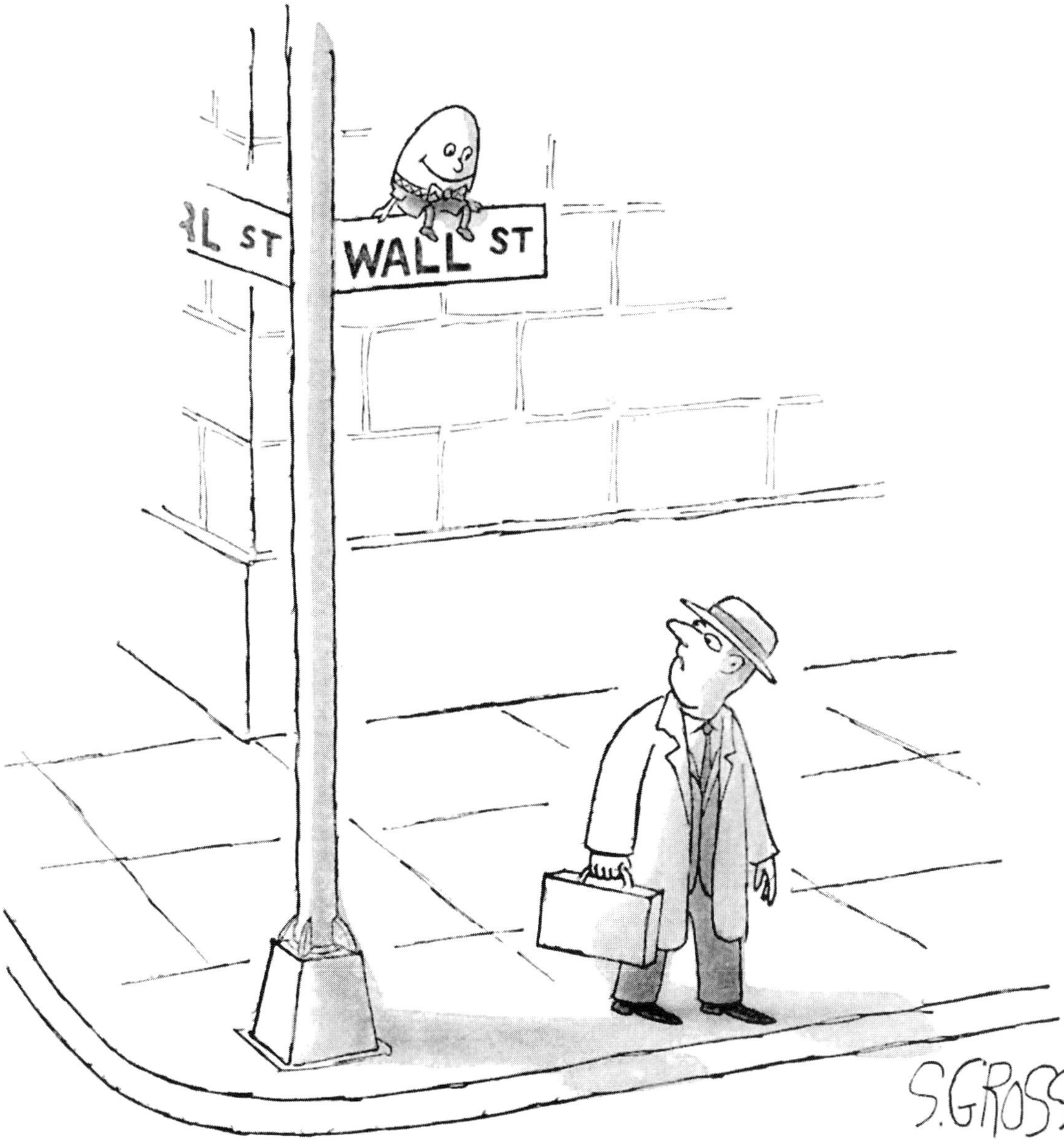

WALL ST
S.GROSS

1980s

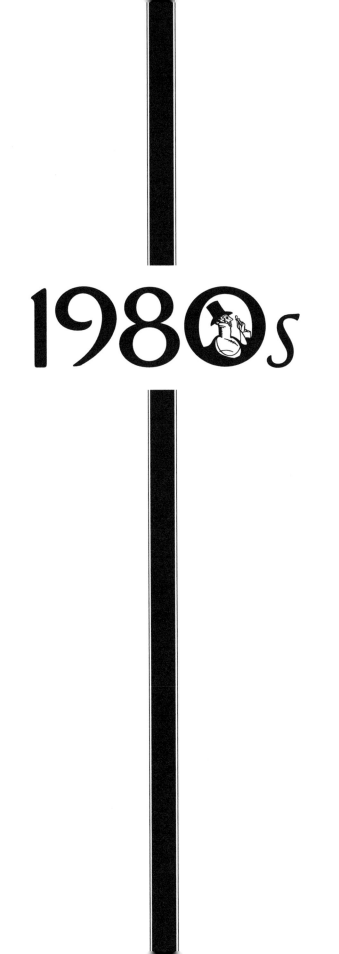

"Liverwurst is down an eighth, egg-salad is up two and a half, and peanut-butter-and-jelly remains unchanged."

"Instead of worrying so much about your <u>money</u> working harder, why don't <u>you</u> work harder?"

"There's a kind of rhythm to making money that something inside me responds to."

"There may be a recession out there, Willie, but there's no recession in here."

"Good evening, Mr. McIlwaine. I'm Mammon."

"The third-largest bank in the country announced today that it would jump off the Brooklyn Bridge. Other banks are expected to follow its example."

"The Clarksons and the Baldwins are old money, the Schaefers and McNallys are new money, the Judds, the Lamberts, the Walters are no money . . ."

"What a delightful surprise.
I always thought it just trickled down to the poor."

"And just why do we always call <u>my</u> income the second income?"

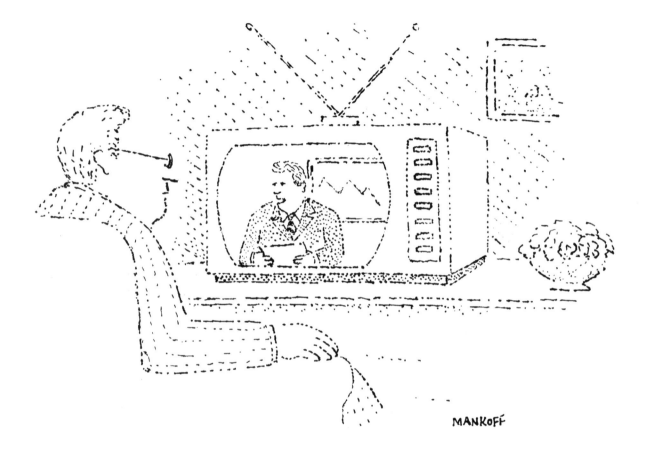

"On Wall Street today, news of lower interest rates sent the stock market up, but then the expectation that these rates would be inflationary sent the market down, until the realization that lower rates might stimulate the sluggish economy pushed the market up, before it ultimately went down on fears that an overheated economy would lead to a reimposition of higher interest rates."

THE ANNEX FUND

LAST MONEY MARKET FOR 8 BLOCKS

*"These projected figures are a figment of our imagination.
We hope you like them."*

1980s

"I suppose it's not *that* much if you see it in the context of a three-trillion-dollar economy."

"Son, you're all grown up now. You owe me two hundred and fourteen thousand dollars."

"Heavens, he's not worrying about <u>his</u> money, he's worrying about money itself."

"You missed the gold play, you missed the real-estate boom and the market upturn, and you're probably missing something else this very minute."

"Oh, sure, I've laid a few. But that was when gold was over seven hundred dollars an ounce."

"Here's the story, gentlemen. Sometime last night, an eleven-year-old kid in Akron, Ohio, got into our computer and transferred all our assets to a bank in Zurich."

"We might make unwise international loans, Mr. Simpson, but we don't make unwise loans to individuals."

TOTAL LOSS PICTURES.®

presents:

I Was a Teen-Age Tax Deduction

Business Trip to the Bottom of the Sea

Beach Blanket Write-Off

May I have a receipt, please?

R. Chast

STEVENSON

"I bet Paul Volcker doesn't worry about interest rates nearly as much as you do."

BEES

WORKER

QUEEN

DRONE

CONSULTANT

MCCRAWFORD

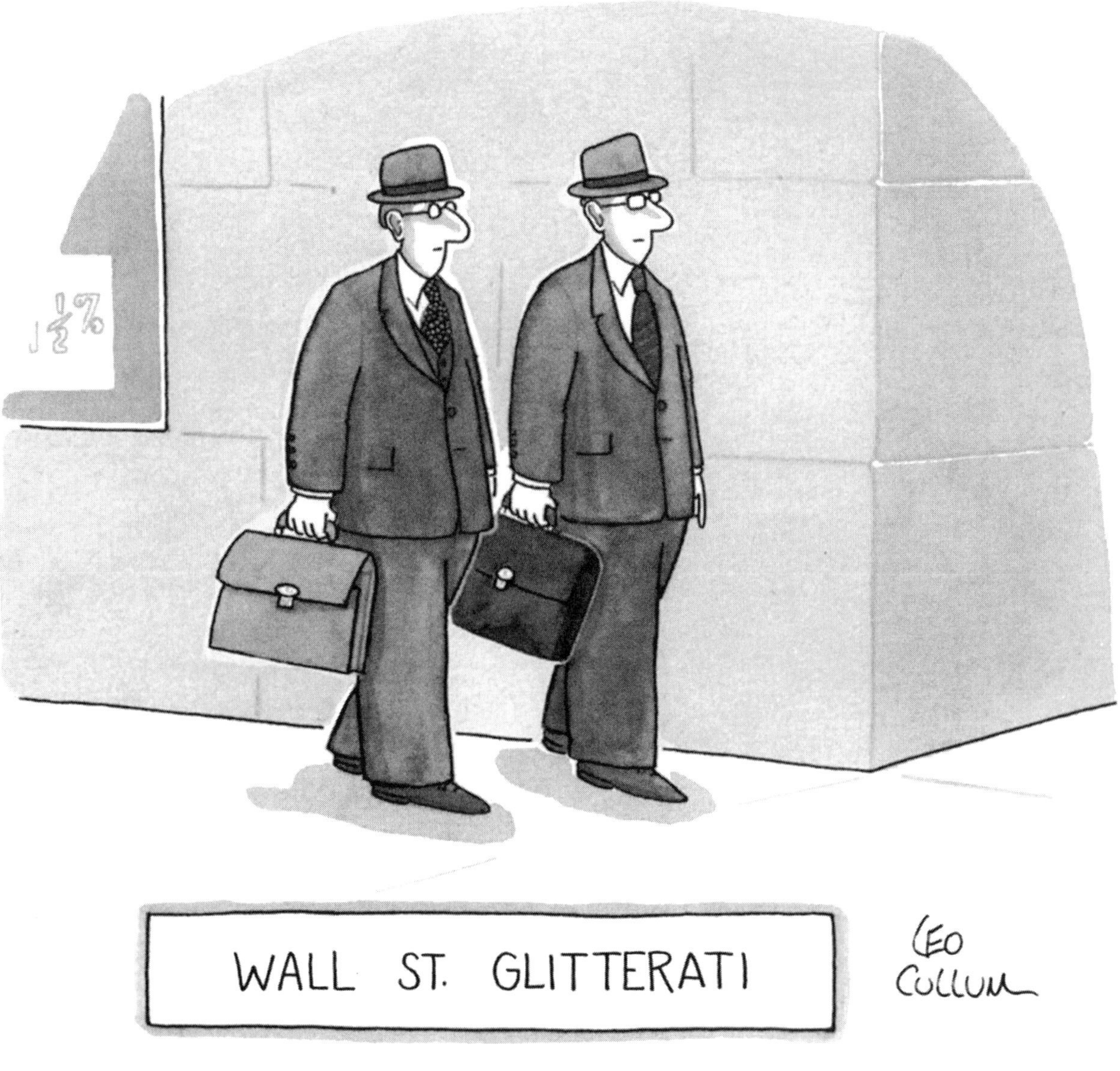
1/2
1 1/2
WALL ST. GLITTERATI
LEO CULLUM

"Bob, as a token of my appreciation for this wonderful lunch I would like to disclose to you my income-tax returns for the past four years."

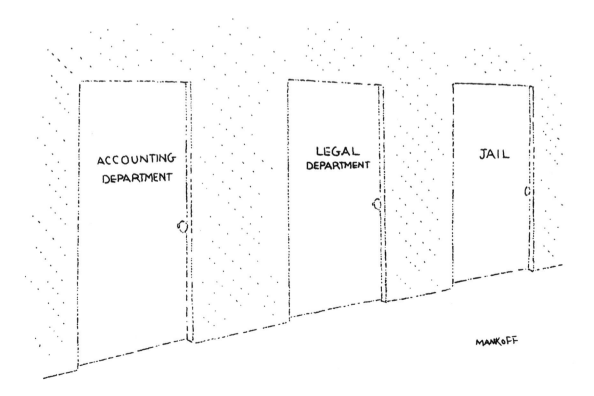

ACCOUNTING DEPARTMENT

LEGAL DEPARTMENT

JAIL

"Every bubblehead with a buck is back speculating in the market again, thank God."

"Where there's smoke, there's money."

*"What I'd like, basically, is a temporary
line of credit just to tide me over the rest of my life."*

"I suppose one could say it favors the rich, but, on the other hand, it's a great incentive for everyone to make two hundred grand a year."

"To wealth, even if it's only on paper."

"It's true, I do have tons of money. But, let's face it, one more ton couldn't hurt."

"You realize, of course, that any attempt on my part to profit by this information would put me at risk of an investigation by the S.E.C."

"Eventually I'd like to have a business where the money rolls in and I wouldn't have to be there much."

"Somewhere out there, Patrick, is the key to increased sales. I want you to find that key, Patrick, and bring it to me."

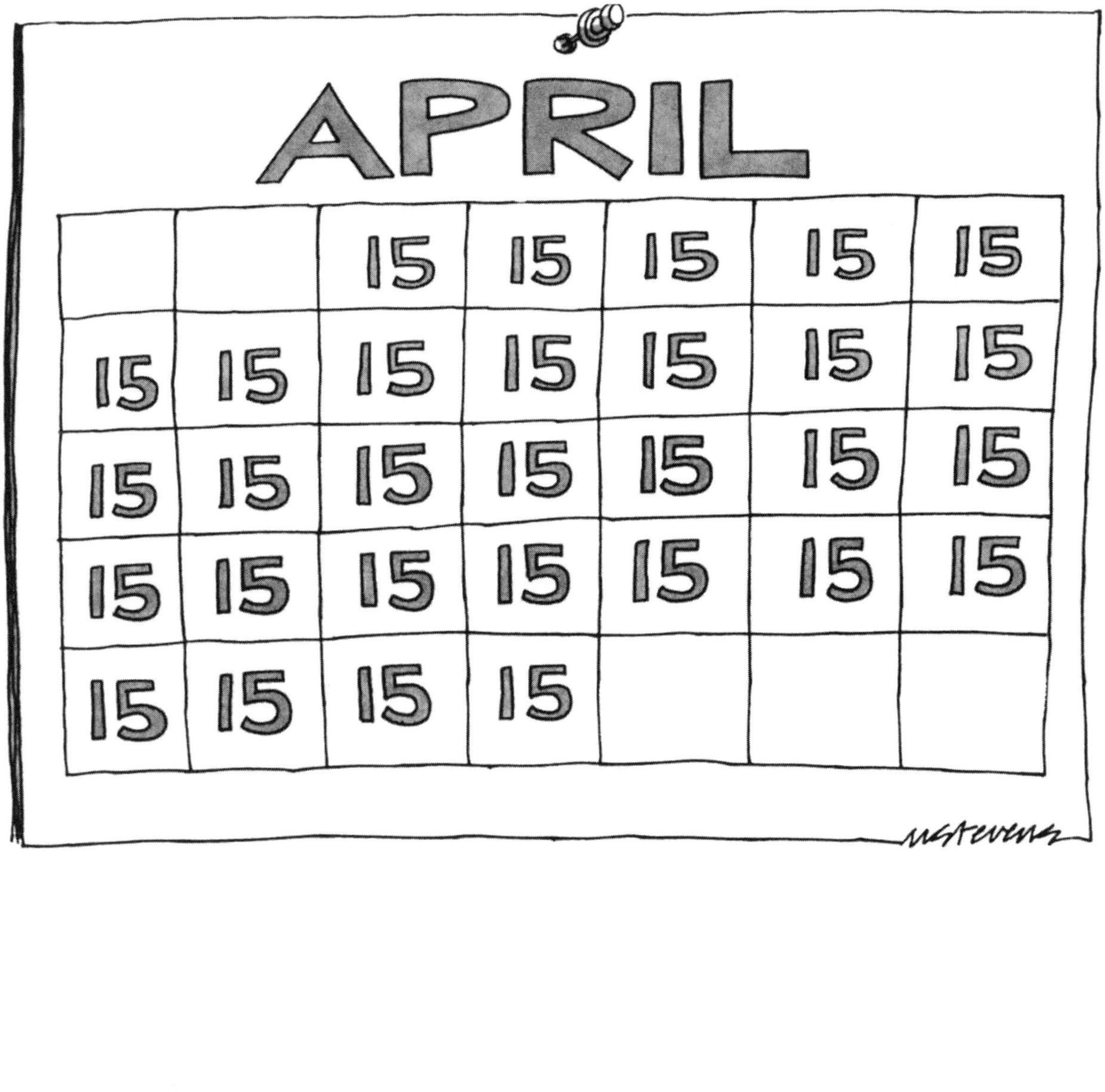
APRIL
15 15 15 15 15
15 15 15 15 15 15 15
15 15 15 15 15 15 15
15 15 15 15 15 15 15
15 15 15 15

"Forty-seven years old and I'm still a small investor."

"We're still pretty far apart. I'm looking for a six-figure advance and they're refusing to read the manuscript."

"This year, tax reform has radically changed the federal tables and methods for calculating witholding taxes."

"Thanks, Pop, but today's kids don't want money, they want leadership."

"Your mother called to remind you to diversify."

"Hi, Dad. Investment banking wasn't that great after all."

*"I just know I'm going to love horses all my life.
That's why I'm planning to have a career in
banking, insurance, and real estate."*

"New money, Bobby, is old money that got away."

"Today the secret ingredients for Mom's Apple Pie were sold to the Japanese for sixty-eight million dollars."

"When you say 'Do we have enough
life insurance?' I assume you mean me."

"We study, we plan, we research.
And yet, somehow, money still remains
more of an art than a science."

"Our deficit-reduction plan is simple,
but it will require a great deal of money."

"'Leverage,' by Goldman, Sachs."

"The chicken is for this year's taxes. The egg is my estimated for next year."

"Mind you, this isn't to be considered a quid pro quo."

"As far as I'm concerned, they can do what they want with the minimum wage, just as long as they keep their hands off the maximum wage."

1990s

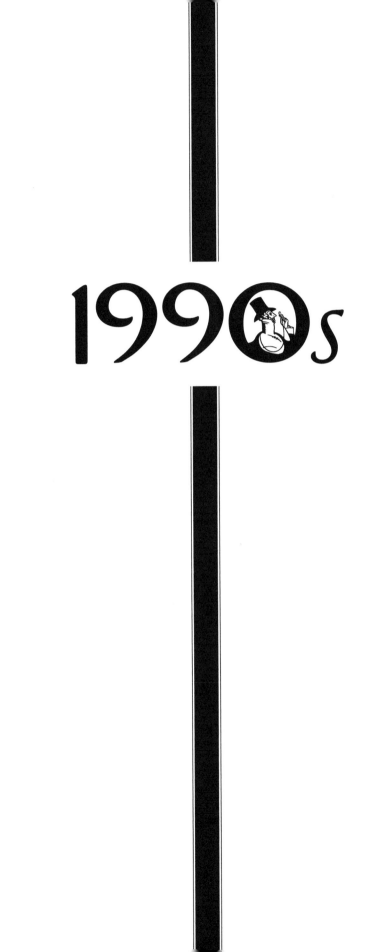

"Welcome aboard. You are now exempt from federal, state, and local taxes."

"Your money was working for you,
but it suddenly quit and now it's working for me!"

"And then, at the height of their power, they seem to have succumbed to a mysterious people known as 'the bottom-line types.'"

"Do you, Scofield Industries, take Amalgamated Pipe?"

"It's a check for a hundred thousand dollars. Do you like it?"

"You drive yourself too hard. You really must learn to take time to stop and smell the profits."

"I'm having an out-of-money experience."

"Gentlemen, yours is going to be one of this period's seminal bankruptcies."

"Incredible, but is it billable?"

"It's up to you now, Miller. The only thing that can save us is an accounting breakthrough."

"O.K., who can put a price on love? Jim?"

"Please stand by for a series of tones. The first indicates the official end of the recession, the second indicates prosperity, and the third the return of the recession."

"It's like this. If the rich have money, they invest. If the poor have money, they eat."

"You're a fine one to talk about _my_ spending!"

"In six more weeks, these M.B.A.s will be ready for market."

"Of course, with the position that has the benefits—medical, dental, et cetera—there is no salary."

"Let's face it—man's best friend is money."

"We are neither hunters nor gatherers. We are accountants."

*"I've always had this dream of buying
a little farm and then selling it off piece by piece."*

"Winning is crucial to my retirement plans."

*"If you would like to receive a guaranteed annual
income of a million dollars or more, press 'one' now."*

"A <u>very</u> special interest to see you, Senator."

"The figures for the last quarter are in. We made significant gains in the fifteen-to-twenty-six-year-old age group, but we lost our immortal souls."

"I'll be honest with you, Jeannette, I'm looking for a no-load relationship."

"I say we go for the record in punitive damages!"

"Millions is craft. Billions is art."

"Will you stop bothering us? We already have a brokerage firm."

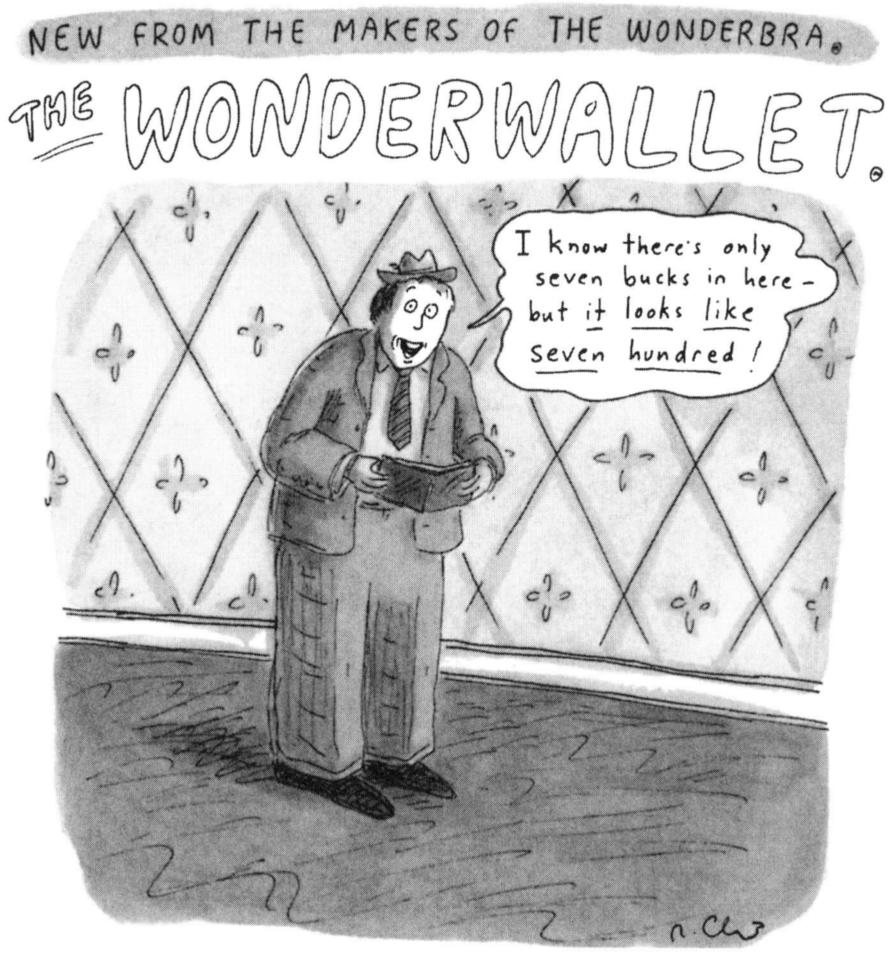
NEW FROM THE MAKERS OF THE WONDERBRA.
THE WONDERWALLET.
I know there's only seven bucks in here - but it looks like seven hundred!

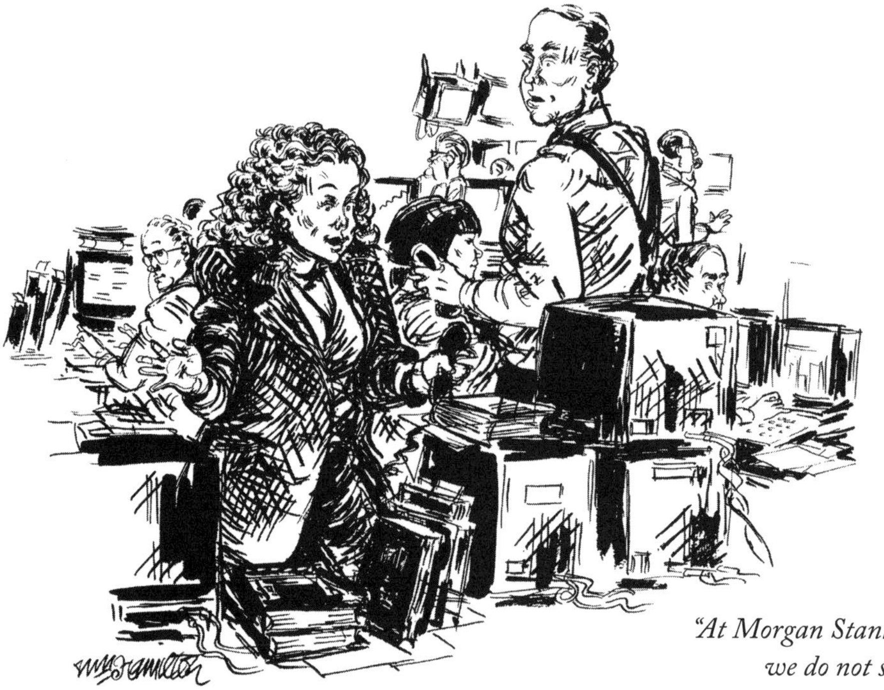

"At Morgan Stanley, Ms. Brimworth, we do not shout 'Bingo!'"

"*People like you don't seem to realize that this precious environment of yours is very expensive to maintain.*"

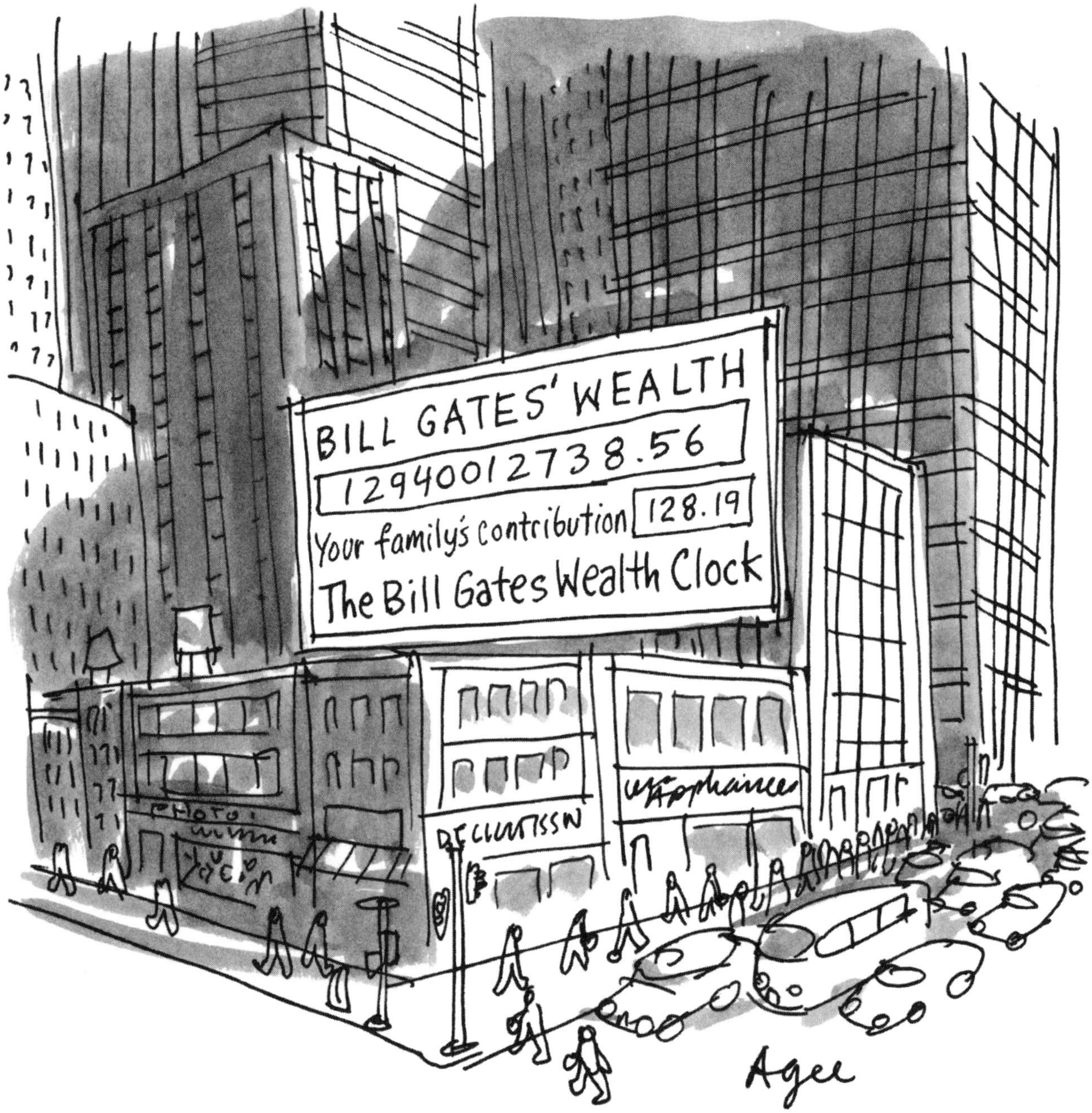
BILL GATES' WEALTH
12940012738.56
Your family's contribution 128.19
The Bill Gates Wealth Clock
Agee

*"A million two does seem a bit heavy for a one-bedroom at first,
but this unit has the best feng-shui in the building."*

"We jacked up our prices to ensure that you
receive the same quality and service in the future."

"Has there been any unusual activity in our stock?
The canary just died."

*"I've never said this to a woman before,
but here goes: We're not paying you enough."*

"I could cry when I think of the years I wasted
accumulating money, only to learn that my cheerful disposition is genetic."

"How come Jasper's mutual fund is up twelve per cent and mine's only up eight?"

"Dad, the dean has gone over your financial statement, and he doesn't think you're working up to your full potential."

"I've been saving this baby for the stock market."

"I was at a high-powered investment firm for seven years and
a high-powered penal institution for a year and a half."

"There, there it is again—the invisible
hand of the marketplace giving us the finger."

"And please let Alan Greenspan accept the things he cannot change, give him the courage to change the things he can and the wisdom to know the difference."

"This is Mr. Harrington, our mortgage nerd."

"No one ever went broke making a profit."

1990s

*"The little pig with the portfolio of straw and the little pig
with the portfolio of sticks were swallowed up, but the little
pig with the portfolio of bricks withstood the dip in the market."*

*"Oh, I'm really sorry. I just placed three million with
some broker who called five minutes ago."*

"Dow Jonesy enough for you?"

"Up a hundred and sixteen points!
If only we'd had the foresight to invest ten minutes ago."

MANKOFF

"I'm looking for a hedge against my hedge funds."

"Hold everything!"

"What do you have in investment-grade reds?"

*"Kids, your mother and I have spent so much money on health insurance this
year that instead of vacation we're all going to go in for elective surgery."*

spare
a
dime?

spare-a-dime?.com

SIPRESS

"*Of course he looks peaceful—he's lived his entire life in a bull market.*"

"Stop complaining. Who isn't broke?"

2000s

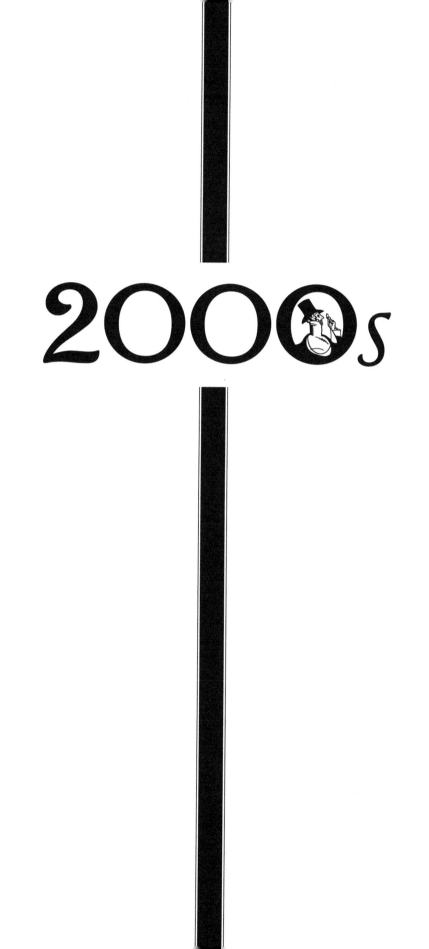

"Captain, it looks like we've entered cyberspace."

"To our divorces—powerful tools
of capital formation."

"Sure, it may be great for us,
but it's hell on the markets."

"I got my ticket for three dollars over the Internet.
Are you going to eat that salmon?"

2000s

"O.K. guys, now lets go and <u>earn</u> that four hundred times our workers' salaries."

"What was it this time, old economy or new economy?"

2000s

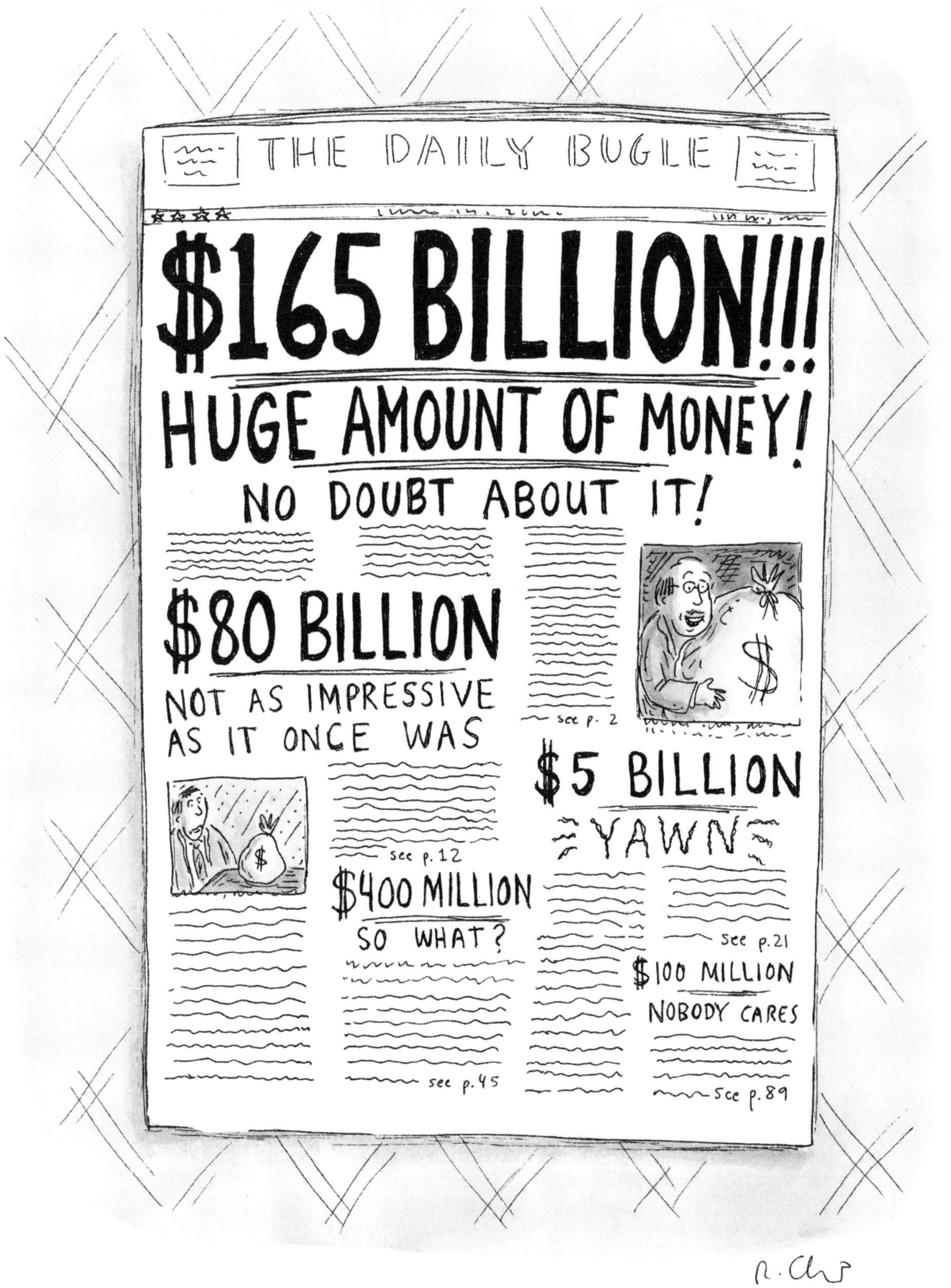
THE DAILY BUGLE
$165 BILLION!!!
HUGE AMOUNT OF MONEY!
NO DOUBT ABOUT IT!
$80 BILLION
NOT AS IMPRESSIVE AS IT ONCE WAS
see p. 2
$5 BILLION
YAWN
see p. 12
$400 MILLION
SO WHAT?
see p. 21
$100 MILLION
NOBODY CARES
see p. 45
See p. 89

"Forgive the mess.
Warren just put everything into cash."

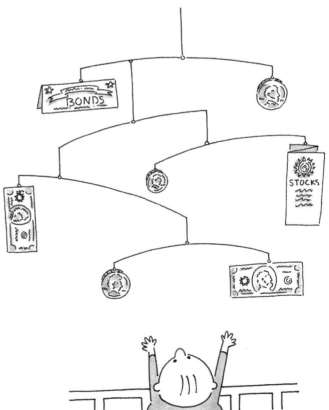

W. BRESSLER

"I, too, hate being a greedy bastard,
but we have a responsibility to our shareholders."

"Hey, I'm just happy to be making an
obscene amount of money."

"Researchers say I'm not happier for being richer,
but do you know how much researchers make?"

"Yes, I do make things, son. I make things called deals."

*"What's to prevent some total stranger anywhere
in the world from paying my bills?"*

"Bad news on Wall Street today, as the bottom fell out of the market, the sides collapsed, and the top blew away."

"Well, we've licked taxes—that just leaves death."

"Would it be possible for you to totally exaggerate how much it will cost and how long it will take, so we'll be pleasantly surprised at the end?"

SIPRESS

GREGORY

"I want my bubble back."

B. Smaller

"They may be your grades,
but they're the return on my investment."

2000s

"Your DNA doesn't match your credit history."

"We are prepared to offer you a compensation package that includes a significant portion of the Western Hemisphere."

2000s

YOUR PORTFOLIO

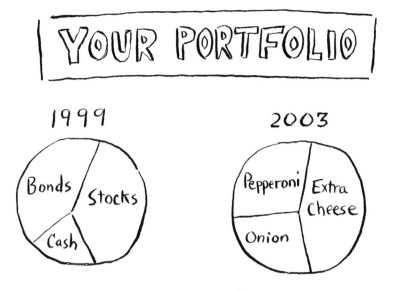

1999

Bonds / Stocks / Cash

2003

Pepperoni / Extra Cheese / Onion

SIPRESS

"On the other hand, their accounting procedures are impeccable."

2000s

"If we take a late retirement and an early death, we'll just squeak by."

"All my lunch money's in real estate."

2000s

"Don't say it never trickled."

*"Now we'll all close our eyes and cover our ears, and the person who took
the four hundred and twenty-eight million dollars will put it back."*

"Where'd you get that?"

"*Mommy usually reads me a story, then slips me a twenty.*"

Means

"I liquidated my assets and put everything into scratch-off lotto."

"Yes, I'm still getting up early, but these days it's to check on the spot markets for oil and natural gas."

"I'm looking for a position where I can slowly lose sight of what I originally set out to do with my life, with benefits."

2000s

"I feel like a man trapped in a woman's salary."

*"It's designed to generate electricity
by moving with fluctuations in the Dow."*

2000s

"I forget—are these your friends where we pretend we make more money than we actually do, or less?"

"I hope we can flip it before the tide comes in."

2000s

"Throw in one of those brochures about refinancing my home."

2000s

"*Try to remember not to mention his obscene bonus.*"

"Oh, what the hell, I'll add another zero."

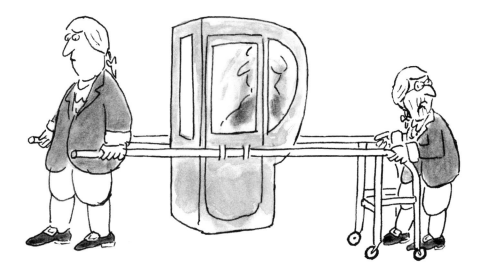

"I can't afford to retire."

S. GROSS

"Run it by legal."   *"Run it by accounting."*

GREGORY

2000s

"Hold it! We almost forgot your backdated stock options."

"If you have to ask how much gas costs, you can't afford it."

"Would you like me to show you around my apartment
and tell you how much I paid for everything?"

"Can you imagine what he would look like without money?"

"The system's not perfect, but, by God, it's transparent."

"Yes, it's nice, but it's lost twenty per cent of its value in the past year."

"God damn it, Kimball—for us, Main Street is Wall Street."

"Not on the mattress where we keep all our money!"

2000s

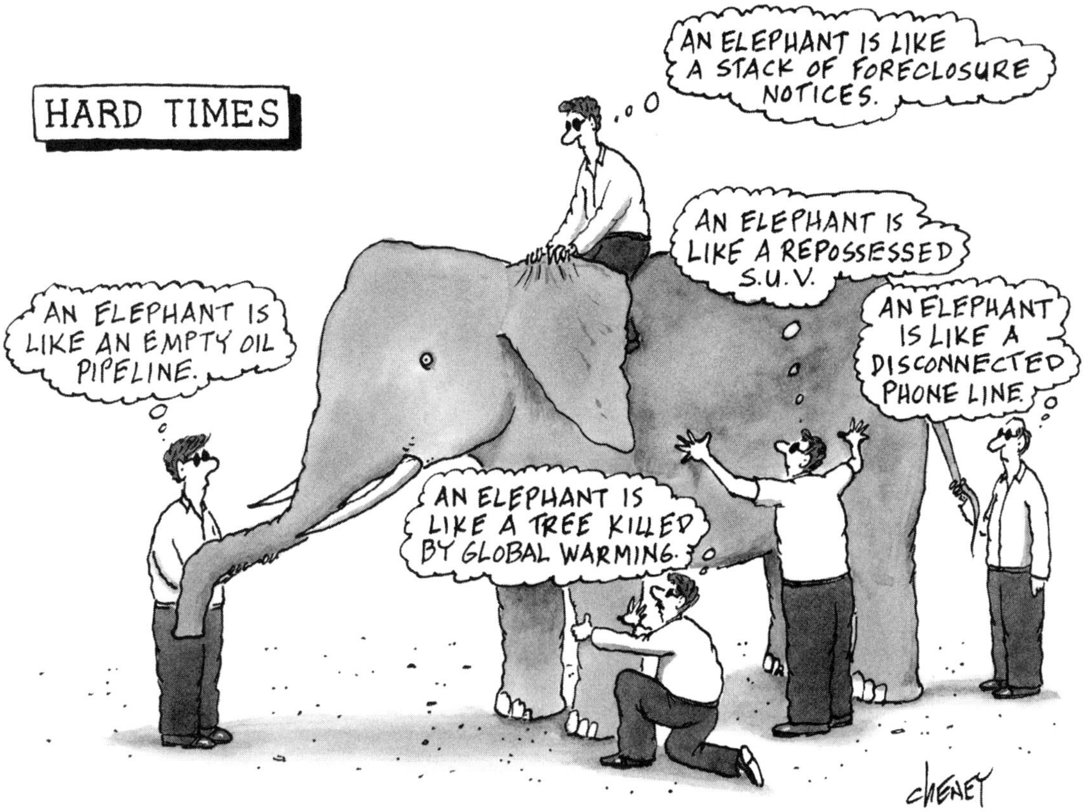
HARD TIMES
AN ELEPHANT IS LIKE A STACK OF FORECLOSURE NOTICES.
AN ELEPHANT IS LIKE A REPOSSESSED S.U.V.
AN ELEPHANT IS LIKE AN EMPTY OIL PIPELINE.
AN ELEPHANT IS LIKE A DISCONNECTED PHONE LINE.
AN ELEPHANT IS LIKE A TREE KILLED BY GLOBAL WARMING.
CHENEY

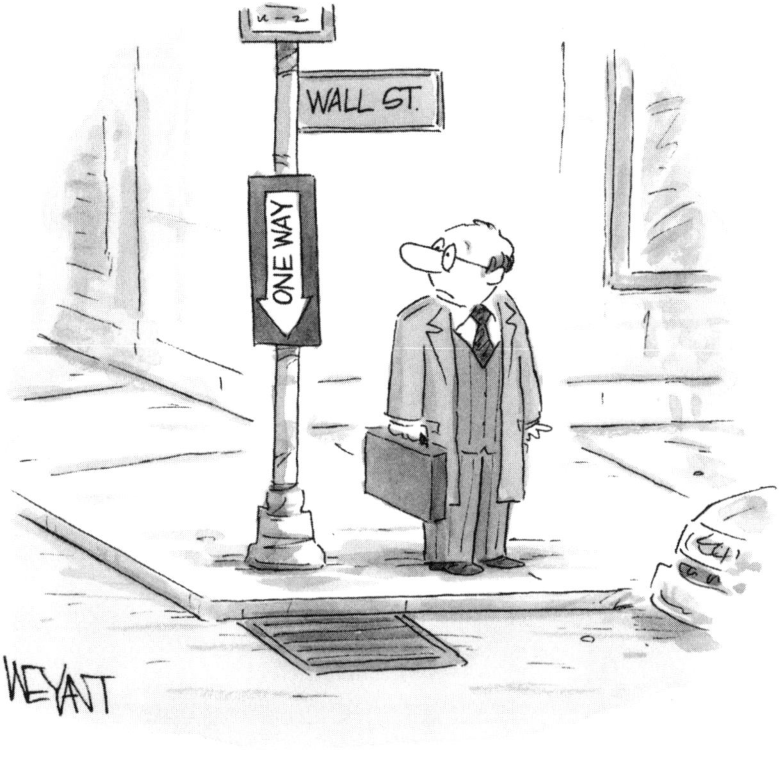
WALL ST.
ONE WAY
WEYANT

"I suppose they'll expect a bailout."

"Hello, son. I suppose chicken farming doesn't seem so bad now."

"Good news. I hear the paradigm is shifting."

DRINKS FOR THE POST-CAFFEINATED ECONOMY

Afternoon Nap

ZZZZZ COLA

DEAD BULL

FIRST NATIONALIZED BANK

"Need anything from the bank?"

"What is it, Lassie—is Timmy in trouble?"

"True, a salary cap on Wall Street may limit the talent pool, but, on the other hand, if they get any more talented we'll all be broke."

MANKOFF

"With these credit default swaps, I never know whose legs I'm supposed to break."

PAUL NOTH

EQUALITY
FRATERNITY LIQUIDITY

2000s

"These new regulations will fundamentally change the way we get around them."

CASH   CREDIT   BARTER

"We're still the same, great company we've
always been, only we've ceased to exist."

INDEX